AMERICAN INDIANS

THE CHICAGO HISTORY OF AMERICAN CIVILIZATION
Daniel J. Boorstin, EDITOR

American Indians
Revised Edition

William T. Hagan

THE UNIVERSITY OF CHICAGO PRESS
Chicago and London

To

WILLIAM F. & VERNA G. HAGAN

The University of Chicago Press, Chicago 60637
The University of Chicago Press, Ltd., London

84 83 82 81 80 79   5 4 3 2 1

ISBN: 0-226-31234-8 (clothbound); 0-226-31235-6 (paperbound)
Library of Congress Catalog Card Number: 78–72176

Table of Contents

List of Illustrations / vii

Editor's Preface / ix

Acknowledgments / xiii

I. Colonial Preparation / 1

II. Foes and Friends / 31

III. Indian Removal / 66

IV. The Warriors' Last Stand / 92

V. Acculturation under Duress / 121

VI. The Indian New Deal and After / 151

Important Dates / 176

Suggested Reading / 179

Index / 187

Illustrations

Facing pages

Cheyenne Horse Travois / 50

Chippewa Hunters / 50

Pawnee Earth Lodge Village / 51

Navaho Woman at Loom / 51

An Arapaho Camp / 82

Zuni Pueblo / 83

Geronimo, His Son and Two Warriors / 130

Cherokee Cabin Home in North Carolina / 130

Winnebago Warriors / 131

Fort Yates Boarding School Kitchen / 162

Blackfoot Reservation Home, 1951 / 162

John Ross / 163

W. W. Keeler / 163

Russell Means, Sioux, 1972 / 170

Dennis Banks, Chippewa, 1972 / 170

Indians Occupying Bureau of Indian Affairs, 1972 / 171

Editor's Preface

It is common to explain one or another feature of American history by the peculiar fact that Europeans transferred their culture to an "empty" continent. The Indians are then recalled, in afterthought, as the people whose presence here prevented the continent from being entirely empty. They are often included with the inclement weather, the wild animals, and the unknown distances, among the half-predictable perils of a wilderness. We are taught to remember them as carrying off an unwary traveler, harassing a wagon train, or fighting the cowboys. The Indians thus seem nothing more than sand in the smoothly oiled gears of American progress.

From the point of view of the Indians themselves, the rise of the United States of America had quite another look. It meant the harassing, the overwhelming, and the extinction of a set of ancient, multiform cultures by a monolithic invasion from far away. We like to contrast our history with that of other empires that arose over the prostrate forms of subject races. Yet in the eyes of other ex-colonial peoples today, the fate of

Editor's Preface

the American Indian seems only a North American version of a drama being played with other actors in Asia and Africa.

In the present volume, Mr. Hagan tells with admirable vividness and brevity the story of the clash of cultures. His focus is not on how the Indians obstructed the progress of American civilization, but on a tragic encounter which was more, not less, tragic because the opposing forces were so unequal. He is not primarily concerned with the internal history of the numerous and diverse Indian communities, but rather with the relations between the Indians and the rising United States. Tracing the different stages in the encounter, and showing the changing attitudes of the predominant new Americans toward the oldest settlers, Mr. Hagan gives us a touchstone for the history of American politics and morals. Familiar episodes of American history take on an unfamiliar look. They become pre-enactments of the dramatic encounter between European peoples and "underdeveloped" countries which has reached a denouement in our own generation.

By relating the story of Indian-white relations to the mainstream of American history, Mr. Hagan makes an important addition to the Chicago History of American Civilization, which aims to make each aspect of our culture a window to all our past. The series contains two kinds of books: a *chronological* group, which provides a coherent narrative of American history from its beginning to the present day, and a *topical* group, which deals with the history of varied and significant aspects of American life. This book is one of the topical group.

Editor's Preface

In perhaps no other subject of American history has the last decade brought more change than in the study of the American Indian. Both descendants of the earlier Indians (who now sometimes insist on not being called "Indians" but simply "native Americans") and descendants of more recently "native" Americans, have revised their points of view. The opportunities for new insight are legion, as are the temptations to passionate overstatement, pride, romanticism, self-flagellation, and polemics. In the revision of this volume. Professor Hagan continues his admirable effort to open new vistas and offer new self-scrutinies of our civilization, while keeping the historian's perspective. He has made changes throughout the volume, has rewritten and updated the final chapter, and has given us a new bibliography, including a selection from the increasingly copious scholarship since his first edition.

In this study Professor Hagan contributes to a large purpose of the Chicago History of American Civilization, which is to remind us of neglected aspects of the civilization that we all share, and to help us understand that, whether our ancestors came here millennia ago or only last year, their experience can and does enrich us all.

DANIEL J. BOORSTIN

Acknowledgments

Grants from the Faculty Research Fund of North Texas State University helped support the preparation of the first edition of this book. Donald J. Berthrong read the first five chapters and saved me from several errors; Hugh M. Ayer read the entire manuscript and was particularly helpful in matters of style. I was assisted in all stages of the enterprise by my wife, Charlotte N. Hagan, and I was fortunate in having the services of two able typists, Mrs. Jonita Borchardt and Mrs. Nana Rylander.

My principal debts for assistance in the revision are to Mrs. Mary Notaro, a cheerful and efficient typist, and to the ever helpful Charlotte N. Hagan.

Colonial Preparation

Nambok the Unveracious, a product of Jack London's literary skill, was a native of the North Pacific Coast who returned unexpectedly to his people after a mysterious disappearance years earlier. After hearing him relate the fantastic ways of the whites with whom he had associated during his absence, the tribe concluded he was either a liar or a spirit returned from the dead and they drove him from their midst.

Shocked incredulity must have been the usual Indian reaction to their initial white contacts. The huge, wind-propelled craft bringing these strangers to their shores could have inspired it. And if the natives were able to master their awe at the size and style of these tremendous canoes, they were astounded by the sight of the great dog-like animals which carried the strangers and their equipment. If in fear of their lives the Indians attempted to drive the invaders back to their boats, they quickly learned to their dismay the superiority of firearms and metal armor over clubs, bows, lances, and leather shields. Subsequent contacts revealed additional miraculous objects to the natives: metal cooking vessels, wheeled transport, sheep, and swine.

The Indians readily learned to use copper kettles and ride horses and eat mutton. Their difficulty lay in their associations with the strangers who had thus enriched their lives. Before many years had passed there were tribes in the South that had encountered Spaniards, Frenchmen, and Englishmen. Along the North Atlantic Coast, Swedes and Dutch had arrived on the scene as well. The confusion of tongues and claims to sovereignty was compounded by the varieties of personality each nation seemed to represent. The Catholic and Protestant missionaries did not agree among themselves, as the Indians came to learn. They, however, clearly had different interests in the Indians than the traders who introduced them to the copper kettles and rum, or the official representatives of the Great Fathers across the waters. The officials talked confusingly of permitting the Indian to occupy land which his tribe had claimed as far back as Indian memory ran, or which the Indian and his fellow warriors had conquered at the risk of their lives.

Over the years closer associations simply deepened the Indians' perplexity. Tenaciously they clung to their own way of life, although they lacked the numbers and disciplined organization to resist the intruders effectively. Over a million Indians occupied the area covered today by the forty-eight states, but the physical and cultural variations were many. Red men came in as many different sizes and shapes and skin tones as the whites who were about to overwhelm them. The only features the Indians had in common were black hair, brown eyes, and some shade of brown skin. The Winnebagos were noted for their large heads; the Utes for their squat, powerful frames; the Crows for their height. These physical variations, coupled with the hundreds of different dialects spoken (although scholars have classified them in six major language groups) offer the best evidence that the migrations from Asia began perhaps 30,000 years ago and included many fragments of Asiatic peoples.

Certainly the white man who had encountered Indian tribes in various parts of the continent had more difficulty in arriving at an "average" Indian than has the producer of the western epics for Hollywood and television. The Chippewa rode in a birchbark canoe, the Chickasaw in a dugout; the Sac slept in a bark wigwam, the Kiowa in a skin tepee, and the Pueblo in a stone apartment house. The Seminole hunted with a blow-gun, the Sioux with a bow. Did this average Indian take his foe's head for a trophy, or did he content himself with just the scalp, and did the scalp include the ears? Did he grow corn, or dig camas roots, or spear salmon? Was boiled puppy a delicacy or a last resort to stave off famine? The Papagos regarded war as a form of insanity, the Comanches gloried in it. The list of variations seemed infinite, and well it might when it is noted that perhaps as many as six hundred different cultures were involved.

Nor did the white man have to travel hundreds of miles to find these cultural variations. The Choctaws and Chickasaws lived side by side, yet the Choctaws were noted for their agricultural skills, the Chickasaws for their belligerency. The Sac and Fox tribes were even more closely allied, but the Sacs were more stable and dependable in political matters. Even within tribes these differences were apparent. Skidi Pawnees were reputed to be better warriors than those from other

Pawnee bands, and the Mohollusha Choctaws were noted for their improvidence as contrasted with other Choctaws. Nor were national characteristics any more permanent among the Indians than among other peoples. A tribe conspicuous for political stability and economic competency might degenerate into a mob of quarreling, drunken brutes within a span of two generations.

Degeneration did not automatically follow tribal associations with the whites. The acquisition of metal tools and utensils, firearms, horses, and sheep simplified life for the Indian. Totem poles and dugouts were more easily fashioned with metal tools, the women fleshed buffalo and deer hides less laboriously with metal scrapers, and they found copper kettles more durable than pottery or woven baskets. Warriors could chisel arrowheads from hoop iron in a fraction of the time required to chip them from flint. Although the early muskets were crude weapons compared with the modern rifle, their superiority over lances and bows and clubs was clearly recognized by the Indian, who cherished the musket which came his way.

Sheep made a new way of life for a few tribes such as the Navaho, but it was the horse which had the greatest impact. For those today classified as plains Indians it facilitated a genuine revolution. Some of them had been primitive agriculturists living on the edge of the plains in permanent villages. Others had been semi-nomadic, but inhibited by their poor transport—dogs carrying packs or dragging travois. As horses drifted north out of the Spanish settlements, being traded from tribe to tribe, or stolen, they produced a new culture for these tribesmen. When these people became mobile, they abandoned their garden patches to follow the buffalo herds. Tepees grew in size and camping equipment became more elaborate as horses were acquired to pull larger travois. An entirely new pattern of life developed, complete with a new religious orientation, new dances, and new games.

Tribes near the plains went through a similar transformation when horses became available to them. The Nez Percé typified those attracted by the new culture. Although some bands remained true to the old ways and subsisted by fishing, root digging, and hunting smaller animals, many Nez Percé now trailed the buffalo herds and borrowed freely from the plains tribes with whom they fought and socialized. They might well have joined the Navahos who denied any pre-horse history: "If there were no horses, there were no Navahos."

Among the eastern tribes, whose forest environment made the horse less valuable, the impact of white culture was still remarkable. With their newly acquired metal files, chisels, needles, knives, and firearms the Indians were able to support themselves with less effort, leaving more time for religious ceremonials, war, and recreation. The old crafts declined and some, like pottery making, became lost arts. But what warrior armed with a trade musket and tomahawk, resplendent in a silk turban and scarlet blanket and jingling silver ear bobs, would be perturbed at this obvious march of progress? Some Indian crafts such as totem pole carving and weaving, challenged by European designs and materials and facilitated by metal tools, achieved new levels of technical excellence. This flurry of creative effort stimulated by the new contacts occurred repeatedly as the white and Indian cultures came into contact.

But not all the tribes enjoyed this renaissance before degeneration set in. For some tribes their first contact with metal weapons came when traditional enemies suddenly appeared so armed and put them to flight. The first two centuries of Indian-white contact produced a prodigious shifting of tribes in response to such pressure. The Iroquois in the East, the Apaches in the Southwest, and the Crees in the Hudson's Bay area were among those Indians who early acquired metal weapons and used them with devastating effects on their neighbors, driving them from choice hunting grounds, seizing their property, enslaving and killing them. The relatively politically sophisticated Iroquois established an empire in New York, Pennsylvania, and the upper Ohio Valley. Crushing the Huron, the Iroquois drove them and other tribes as far west as Wisconsin. When Pawnees ventured east of the Mississippi to raid tribes subject to the Iroquois, these liege lords dispatched war parties nearly a thousand miles to teach the Pawnees a lesson.

As the tribesmen increased their holdings of firearms, metal traps, blankets, and other trade items, they became dependent upon the whites. La Salle recognized this relationship when he commented, "The savages take better care of us French than of their own children; from us only can they get guns and goods." A delay in the arrival of traders with gunpowder and muskets could put the Indians at the mercy of their enemies and the elements. Bourbon ambitions in Europe could produce tragic repercussions for tribesmen in the Mississippi Valley who had never heard of the court at Versailles but whose supply lines ran back to France, while their rivals were supplied by the English. Thus the fortunes of individual tribes ebbed and flowed because of factors they could neither control nor comprehend.

From King William's War in the late seventeenth century

through the War of 1812, tribal allegiances were frequently dictated by the trade situation. At a given moment a tribe might prefer its French or English Father, but if he could not put traders in their villages and his rival could, it had no alternative but to support the rival. Most Indians could not even repair a broken musket; they had to have access to traders. To return to the old way of life would be as easy for them as it would be for the average twentieth-century Manhattanite to convert to dirt farming.

Not infrequently the forerunner of the new way of life would be one of the white man's diseases which swept Indian villages, sometimes almost annihilating tribes and scattering the panic-stricken survivors. Tuberculosis, syphilis, measles, and smallpox were the principal diseases the whites inflicted on the Indian population. The Pilgrims regarded it as divine intervention that some disease, possibly smallpox left by sailors who had visited the area, had slashed eastern Massachusetts' Indian population shortly before the Pilgrims' arrival. The Cherokee medicine men attributed the smallpox epidemic which swept their nation in the 1730's to the sexual lapses of their young people, and some conservative Indians blamed the plagues on the departure from the old ways. In the next century the white man's diseases were still at work solving the Indian problem.

From the beginning there was no unanimity in the white approach to the Indian problem. The French were primarily concerned with the fur trade, and it was to their advantage to make use of the Indian's special skills as a hunter. The possibility of precious metals lured the Spanish into the area that now comprises the United States, but for the Indian the mission became the principal Spanish institution. The English sought Indian land, although the fur trade also attracted some.

The net effect of the evolving policies was most disastrous for those Indians in contact with the English. The Frenchman actually needed the Indian and cultivated him accordingly. The Spanish mission might resemble a forced-labor system and its paternalism was not designed to prepare the mission Indian for independent status in a white society, but it did preserve his life and provide a rude plenty. Although citizens of neither of these Latin Catholic nations had the pronounced racialist views of the Anglo-Saxon, discrimination did exist in Spanish America. The universities were restricted to the whites, an Indian priest was a rarity, and laws were enacted to keep horses and firearms in the hands of whites.

The average English colonist was a farmer, not a fur trader or priest, and to him the Indian was either a nuisance or a menace. If the Indian had departed peacefully, probably racial prejudice would have been only so great as to rationalize ex-propriating him. But he did resist and his style of warfare, braining infants against trees and torturing captives, horrified Englishmen. As a result, some assimilation did take place, but not to the degree nor with the approbation that it took place among the Spanish and French.

One fundamental problem for all colonial powers was land title. Spanish experts like Franciscus de Victoria advised that the Indian title was valid. In contrast, the Swiss jurist Vattel held that the Indian title depended upon their use of the land. Among the English colonies Vattel's view prevailed and what was generally held to have been transferred by treaty was the Indian usufruct, or right to use the land. In negotiating with each other and pre-empting for their national governments the authority to purchase land, all nations maintained the right of discovery to be paramount. In practice the results were essentially the same: if the whites needed the land, they took it.

Compared to Spanish and French, English policy was necessarily confused and contradictory, since the individual colonies contended with each other and the crown in the area of Indian affairs. One of the few unifying threads was the work among Indians sponsored by the infrequent missionary groups which did not take colonial boundaries into account. The colonial charters frequently carried a clause enjoining the grantees to convert and civilize the Indians, but, because the grantees were not investing their money for that purpose, these injunctions had little effect. The missionary impulse was not strong among Englishmen, and the tribesmen did not convert easily. One of the early missionaries gave up in disgust after three years, despairing, "Heathen they are & heathen they will remain."

In authorizing the colonization of Virginia, James I had urged the propagation of the Christian religion among the Indians. Down to the outbreak in 1622 this seems to have received more than just lip service. The Virginia Company officials directed their governor at Jamestown to use force if necessary to separate the Indian children from the unholy atmosphere of their families. Money was appropriated to educate young Indians in Virginia homes and a few were even sent to England, but little progress was made and an uprising in 1622 ended plans for two Indian schools.

The uprising forced a general reorientation of Virginia Indian policy. Virginians had assumed that in time the Indians would recognize the beneficence of civilization. The marriage of John Rolfe to Pocahontas, daughter of Powhatan, who headed the Indian confederation in eastern Virginia, had been expected to consolidate the alliance, particularly after James I, by proxy, had crowned Powhatan. But Powhatan died in 1618 and under his successor, Opechancanough, the Indians united to avenge themselves for the petty slights inflicted by the whites and to eliminate this growing menace to their territory. Although the Virginians beat off these first onslaughts, peace did not return for twelve years.

During that period the Virginia Indian policy was reoriented. The optimistic approach of coexistence disappeared in a welter of ambushes and truce violations. During the remainder of the seventeenth century the only provision for education of Indian students was for those held hostage or captive. As the Reverend Samuel Purchas rationalized Virginia's new policy, the Indian had broken natural law and was no longer entitled to consideration.

The uneasy peace was broken in 1644 by a last concerted effort to drive the Virginians into the ocean. Led again by Opechancanough, now so enfeebled by age he had to be carried on a litter, the tribesmen killed about five hundred whites in the surprise attacks that opened the war. The survivors quickly rallied and easily crushed the Indian forces. The buildup of strength in the settlements had reached the point that without outside help the Indians could not win a protracted war. For a century and a half the war whoop echoed on the Virginia frontier and captives returned to tell ghastly stories of torture and enslavement, but after Opechancanough's defeat the destined victor was obvious. For the frontiersmen the threat was very real, but for the whole colony the Indian constituted little more than a nuisance.

Before the Virginia Indians drifted into obscurity they were counseled to send some of their young men to the College of William and Mary, which had a few Indian students supported by charity and instructed in segregated classes. A spokesman declined, explaining that their young men who had been exposed to the white man's education had returned bad runners, ignorant of woodcraft, susceptible to cold and hunger, "neither fit for hunters, warriors, nor counsellors." He did offer to make men of any Virginia youths sent to the Indians for instruction. There is no record that Virginia officially availed itself of the opportunity, but generations of frontiersmen traded boots for moccasins and excelled their tutors at scalping.

The other southern colonies profited from Virginia's experience in Indian affairs. Maryland authorities were fortunate in not having to contend with a confederation as powerful as Opechancanough's, and they were more careful to leave the tribes with some feeling of compensation. The Jesuits who followed Lord Baltimore to Maryland apparently hoped to launch large-scale mission enterprises comparable to those of Spanish colonies, but discovered that Baltimore's religious zeal was not sufficient to tolerate this threat to his proprietorship.

For Carolina and Georgia, trade and imperial defense were the determining factors in their Indian relations. By 1750 Charleston was the center of the fur trade in the South and an estimated 1,250,000 deerskins passed through that port between 1739 and 1759. Trade of this volume attracted competition and the southern colonies were frequently at odds since Virginia traders ignored South Carolina regulations.

Farther south, Georgia's early Indian relations were relatively painless owing to Oglethorpe's prestige with the Creeks. Recognizing the power of this tribe he courted their favor through Mary, a half-blood Creek woman who married successively a South Carolina trader, a Georgia militia officer, and a former Indian agent turned cleric. All of Mary's husbands, as well as Oglethorpe, profited from Mary's relation to the head of the Creek nation. These white men were not the first, nor the last, to use Indian marriages to further their economic and political objectives. Sentiment may have played a role in these connections, but it is interesting to note that white men usually contracted such liaisons only with close relatives of tribal leaders.

No such intermarriage eased the movement of the Pilgrims and Puritans into New England, but they had something far better—the assurance that God was on their side. Through the agency of the plague He had cleared the way for His chosen people and this morally justified the Pilgrims' refusal to purchase the land from the Indians. Whether at Plymouth or the settlements around Massachusetts Bay, the settlers had little difficulty identifying the Indians as agents of Satan. It required no great change in Puritan mentality to make room in their universe, already peopled with witches and saints, for these "tawney serpents" and "hideous creatures."

There were exceptions. The Pilgrims were delighted to have the advice and fellowship of Squanto. Speaking English he had learned from slave traders, Squanto served as an intermediary between the neighboring tribes and the Pilgrims, besides introducing them to native foods like planked shad and the clambake.

Roger Williams and John Eliot did not fit the pattern either. Eliot denounced his fellow Puritans for their enslavement of Indians and neglect of their missionary responsibilities. He translated the Bible into a local Indian dialect and helped establish several reservations of Christian or "praying" Indians.

Colonial Preparation

Roger Williams was even more heretical in New England eyes. He attacked the Puritan policy of recognizing Indian rights to land only if it were occupied by villages or under cultivation. He insisted the Indians also had a valid title to their hunting grounds.

Any debate over Indian claims to land became purely academic after the Pequot War of 1637. One of the few tribes whose strength was unimpaired by the plague, the Pequots chose to resist the movement of settlers into the Connecticut Valley. At night a small party of whites surrounded the Pequot stronghold, fired it, and over five hundred Indians were killed or burned to death, while the attackers lost but two men. The remnants of the tribe were sold into slavery. The Narragansetts, wooed by Roger Williams, had provided an auxiliary for the white squads that combed the woods for surviving Pequots. Such help was badly needed by the whites in 1637 for some of their commanders continued to think in terms of warfare as it was waged in Europe. White captains had to learn and relearn the lesson that Indian fighting required speed and stealth rather than cumbersome baggage trains and troops maneuvering in ranks in open country.

The Puritans confidently attributed their victory over the Pequots to divine intervention. One of their captains said it was "as though the finger of God had touched both match and flint," and that the Indian cries, as they succumbed to the flames and bullets, were so pathetic that "if God had not fitten the hearts of men for the service, it would have bred in us a commiseration towards them." Increase Mather called upon his congregation to thank God, "that on this day we have sent six hundred heathen souls to hell."

Three decades elapsed before the next Indian crisis in New

England, King Philip's War, 1675–76. Sparked by the Wampanoag chief Philip, it was a coalition war aimed originally at Plymouth. The usual disregard for Indian personal and property rights, attempts to enforce Indian observance of the Puritan Sabbath, and a legal code providing capital punishment for blasphemy, furnished Philip allies from the Narragansetts. Three tribes, however, furnished auxiliaries for the New Englanders. Once again the Indian allies of the whites at least shortened the war if they did not completely alter its course.

The war did tax the resources of New England to the limit. A score of settlements were wiped out and the death toll ran over a thousand. Finally victorious, the whites bloodily avenged themselves. Philip was captured, drawn and quartered; his skull remained on view on a pole in Plymouth as late as 1700. The Narragansett chief Canonchet was also captured and sentenced to be beheaded. Informed of his fate he remarked stoically that he was happy to go "before his heart was soft, or he had spoken anything unworthy of himself." Hundreds of Indians captured were not executed but sold into slavery, many of them to the West Indies. This not only rid the country of surplus Indian population but helped defray some of the expenses of the war. The Puritan conscience was not troubled by this slave traffic. The Indians were simply the agents of Satan, successful to the degree that the Puritans had strayed from grace by leniency to the Quakers or by the obsession of Puritan wives and daughters with the "cutting, curling and immodest laying out of their hair."

The Indians, as usual following one of these wars, went downhill rapidly. Brought under close surveillance, the recently hostile and friendly tribesmen alike were required to live in specified villages, arms and ammunition were denied them, and precautions were taken against their assembling. Plymouth authorities even revived the Anglo-Saxon tithing system by making one Indian in each group of ten responsible for the behavior of the others.

In semi-isolation, the New England Indians did what countless generations of tribesmen were to do later on reservations from the Atlantic to the Pacific: they degenerated. Unable to revert to their primitive practices, they picked up the white man's vices and diseases faster than they acquired his virtues. The proposition that contact with the whites corrupted rather than uplifted was demonstrated all too well in the Puritan theocracy.

The pattern of events in the middle colonies was similar to that in New England and the South. The Dutch and Swedes pioneered in that area and had virtually cleared southern New York and New Jersey of Indians by the time the English supplanted them. Governor Kieft of New Amsterdam is credited with offering the first bounty for Indian scalps, a more convenient trophy than heads. The Dutch resembled the English more than the French in their relations with their Indian neighbors. They did not dignify their relations with Indian women by marriage, and they exhibited the same lack of missionary zeal. As traders, however, they were very effective and after scattering the smaller tribes on the lower Hudson effected a mutually profitable relationship with the Iroquois which the English inherited.

The fame of the Iroquois had spread far and wide. In 1682, William Penn dispatched a letter to the "Emperor of Canada," as he addressed the ranking chief of the Iroquois, apprising him of the Quaker intention to develop Pennsylvania. Although they failed ultimately to produce a society in which the Indian could live as an equal, the Pennsylvania Quakers compiled a record of just dealings with the tribesmen clearly superior to that of the other colonists. Penn was careful to purchase Indian land claims, his first treaty on the banks of the Delaware being described by Voltaire as the only treaty not sealed by an oath, and the only treaty kept faithfully by the whites. But gradually the white pressure on Indian lands and the necessity of propitiating the dangerous Iroquois led to the expulsion of the Delawares and other small tribes from southeastern Pennsylvania. The wealthy Quaker merchants of Philadelphia were not as ruthless as the Scotch-Irish on the frontier; however, they were a far cry from George Fox and William Penn, as their behavior in the intense rivalry for the Indian trade indicated.

For the Indians this rivalry was a mixed blessing. Competition did bring higher prices for their furs, but cutthroat rivalry led to the wholesale introduction of rum and debauchery of entire tribes. Traders employed any tactics to make an immediate profit on the assumption that next year they might be crowded out. As the trade wars multiplied, and tribal rivalries were encouraged for trade purposes, they resulted in the virtual extermination of some tribes and the expulsion of others. These conditions were only intensified when the competition was between French and English, or Spanish and English traders, instead of between Georgians and South Carolinians.

These international trade rivalries provided one of the chief motivations for the struggle for control of North America. Granted that the four great wars waged between 1689 and 1763 (King William's, Queen Anne's, King George's, and the French and Indian) had their origins in European politics, they frequently did no more than give official status to what was already going on along the frontier. French and English traders contending for the furs harvested by the tribes did not need a declaration of war to recognize a state of hostility. They were continually intriguing with the tribesmen to hold the trade they had and to undercut their competition.

Although the Iroquois were sufficiently powerful to play the role of a balance of power on the New York–Canadian frontier, the average tribe simply responded to the nation able to bring the most power to bear upon it. True, the Indian found the Frenchmen less race-conscious and less covetous of Indian land, but English trade goods were generally cheaper and superior in quality. Both sides employed Indian auxiliaries. The French were dependent on them for their offensive punch because French troops were too few to be more than a stiffener for the war parties which devastated the frontier of the English colonies. Neither the French nor the English could operate in the trackless forests without Indian scouts and guides.

The aftermath of a raid on Haverhill, Massachusetts, indicates the nature of the warfare. Spurred on by indications of the treatment awaiting them in the Indian villages, two captive white women and a boy tomahawked ten of a party of twelve Indian men, women and children while they slept during a break on the trail to Canada. Hannah Dustin, one of the women, then scalped their victims and returned to Haverhill with her bloody trophies and claimed the bounty offered by the colonial government.

The Indian casualty rates in these campaigns were high. In the South the Spanish mission system among the Florida Indians never recovered from the raids of the English and their Indian allies who killed and enslaved the Spanish wards. The white man's wars and need for slaves were pitting the Indians against each other and only the whites could be the winner. One agent described the tactic as setting one wolf pack against another.

The record indicates the Indians were beginning to perceive the folly of exterminating each other for the benefit of the white men. On the New York frontier the Iroquois had learned well the advantages of neutrality and were inclined to play off the French against the English. The Six Nations sat out Queen Anne's War. Pressed by crown representative William Johnson, only late in King George's War did the Iroquois leave their long houses to plague the French and their Indian allies.

Interested initially in the Indian trade, Johnson became the spokesman for imperial Indian policy after his appointment as Indian commissioner. More like a Frenchman than an Englishman in his relations with the Indians, Johnson had children by several Indian women. The best known of these women was Mary Brant, member of a prominent Mohawk family and a clan matron.

Iroquois power declined as the French and English competition moved into the Ohio Valley in the 1730's and 1740's. French control of the western Great Lakes and the Mississippi gave them an early advantage, but the hostility of the Foxes sapped the strength of the French. Their competition for trade came largely now from Virginians and Pennsylvanians spearheaded by aggressive men like George Croghan, a young Irishman who sought to make his fortune in the Indian trade. When war came in 1744, the Ohio Indians were persuaded by their English traders to attack the French. Through Croghan even the Quaker-dominated Pennsylvania government was induced to support the Indians against the French. The extent of Pennsylvania's aid, however, did not satisfy the tribesmen.

Colonial Preparation

One delegation to Philadelphia reminded the whites that they had involved the Indians in this war and should support them more liberally with arms and ammunition. "And we are now come to tell you that French have hard Heads," the Indian orator complained, "and that we have nothing strong enough to break them. We have only little Sticks & Hickeries. . . ." The Quaker support was small and grudgingly given, but it did help keep some of the Ohio Indians in the English camp. The Ohio Valley was to be the scene of the most intense French-English rivalry in the years between King George's War and the French and Indian War.

Alarmed at the infiltration of the English into an area they had regarded as their own and unable to compete with English liberality, the French resorted to force. In 1749 one French detachment traveled down the Allegheny and the Ohio warning English traders away and trying in vain to get the tribes to expel the Englishmen from their villages. Three years later another French column surprised the Miami village of Pickawillany, captured five English traders, confiscated their goods, and killed a number of Indian allies of the English. As a salutary lesson to other Ohio tribesmen the French Indian auxiliaries boiled and ate the Miami chief.

Refusing to be intimidated, the pro-English tribes prepared to resist the French strong-arm methods. But when the Indians looked to the English for leadership and supplies the colonists demonstrated their chronic disunity. Virginians were at odds with Pennsylvanians over trade in the Ohio Valley, the governor of South Carolina resented the governor of Virginia giving gifts to southern Indians, and Pennsylvanians were embroiled with New Yorkers over the Lake Erie trade. And there were struggles within colonies. Governor Dinwiddie of Virginia, an aggressive executive who was financially interested in the Ohio Company, tried to use it as an agency to extend English power and lost the co-operation of other Virginians with different financial interests. In New York, traders at Oswego advocated different policy for the Iroquois from that proposed by traders at Albany.

Some British officials accused the Iroquois of becoming soft on the French issue. French traders and Catholic priests had made substantial headway within the confederacy, which was increasingly impressed with the advantages of neutrality. Alarmed at the drift of events, the Board of Trade in London requested that seven of the colonies most concerned send delegates to a conference to be held in Albany in the summer of 1754 for the purpose of improving relations with Iroquois and strengthening colonial defenses.

The Albany Conference was a disappointment to its sponsors. The large Iroquois delegation made no commitments and defended their past conduct by reference to the English inability to defend either themselves or their Indian allies. Franklin's Plan of Union inspired no enthusiasm despite his argument that the English colonies should at least be able to do as well as "Six Nations of ignorant savages." But the delegates were too busy trying to outwit each other in land transactions with the Indians to heed the Philadelphia sage. The conference called to organize a united front simply produced more disunity.

Badgered by speculators to sell land, pressed by French traders on the one hand and English on the other, the Indians found their position increasingly intolerable. As an Iroquois spokesman plaintively expressed it, "we don't know what you Christians, English and French together intend; we are so hemmed in by both, that we have hardly a hunting place left. . . . We are so perplexed . . . that we hardly know what to say or think." Their French father spoke with but one tongue, whereas the Virginia and Pennsylvania governors represented only two of several tongues which enunciated English policy.

Attempting to remedy this obvious defect, the Board of Trade recommended a single Superintendent of Indian affairs, but responsibility was divided between William Johnson for the North and Edmund Atkin for the South. Nevertheless, this definitely improved the English handling of Indian affairs at a crucial time, because in the French and Indian War the role of the red men would again be significant. General Braddock's defeat was attributed to his own lack of Indian auxiliaries and the success of the French in winning allies among the western Indians. These numbered perhaps as many as 800 of the 900-man force responsible for the destruction of the British army. George Croghan stated that if Braddock had had fifty Indians scouting for him instead of a mere eight, he would not have been ambushed.

In still other engagements the Indian role was decisive. About the time that Braddock was being cut down, William Johnson was earning his baronetcy at the head of a mixed force of English and Iroquois which blunted a French thrust under Baron Dieskau, whose Indian allies betrayed him into Johnson's ambush. Despite this act of treachery, French commanders continued to bolster their inferior forces with Indian auxiliaries. Inevitably, such methods of warfare produced incidents like that at Fort William Henry when the Indians got out of hand and massacred English troops who had surrendered under a pledge of safe conduct.

This type of warfare, brutal by English standards, was carried to the settlements of central New York and elsewhere along the frontier by raiding parties of French and Indians. All the horrors of previous wars were re-enacted. Outlying settlements were looted and burned, their inhabitants mutilated and killed, or carried into captivity which they might not survive. Only the strong and the lucky made it to Canada. Laggards and complainers were casually tomahawked and, according to contemporary accounts the Indians took a fiendish delight in torturing parents by abusing their children in their presence. Accounts abound of children dashed against tree trunks or scalped and dismembered before their anguished parents. For those who survived the trail to Canada the gantlet might be waiting. Stripped of their clothes and forced to run through lines of Indians armed with clubs and knives, many of the captives died in the ordeal. Or they might survive to undergo some refined torture devised by the Indians to test the hardiness of their prisoners or to furnish psychological compensation for the tribe's loss of valuable fighting men.

The scourge of Indian warfare did not strike western Pennsylvania and Virginia until after Braddock's defeat. The tribesmen in the upper Ohio Valley had not played a significant role in the French victory, many of them being pro-English. With the French now in undisputed control of the region, the Indians had no alternative but to co-operate with them. This transfer of loyalties was made easier by their remembrance of past English abuses—fraudulent land transactions, unscrupulous traders, and occasional acts of physical violence. Some economic determinists have attributed the switch in Indian loyalties to the large debts they had run up to English traders.

By 1758 it was becoming obvious that the Indians, for whatever reason, had picked the wrong side. The British preponderance in troops increased with the arrival of every convoy, while the French were unable to get substantial reinforcements or goods for the Indian trade through the English blockade. Moreover, the western Indians were difficult to maintain for extended duty so far from home and those from the upper Ohio Valley declined to fight for the French who had supplied them with "hardly a loaf of bread." Deserted by their Indian auxiliaries, the French could only retreat in the face of Forbes's army after first blowing up Fort Duquesne.

Three years before the war officially closed, the French had been defeated in Canada, and in the South the same trend had set in. The Creeks and Cherokees took up the hatchet against the English only to be soundly defeated, the Cherokee losses including half of their warriors. The war ended with the French ousted from North America and a feeble Spain holding on in Louisiana. For the Indians the war had had catastrophic results. Not only had some tribes suffered grievous losses, but their power to bargain was destroyed as was apparent by 1759 in the new tone of British Indian policy. As one of the British officers observed, "We can now talk to our new Allies in a proper Stile, as their Services are not Necessary."

Lord Jeffrey Amherst, who headed the British military forces in North America from 1758 to 1763, was an experienced and meticulous soldier, but a poor hand with Indians. Ignorant of their character, he proposed to handle the red men as he handled the red-coated battalions of the British army. Amherst's plans called for a reduction of expenditures in the Indian service, a return of all white captives held by the tribesmen, and a resumption of the fur trade. To economize and to force the Indians to hunt, he curtailed the gift-giving which had become an institution when the French and English bid for the Indian's favor. The stern general summed it up neatly: "When men of what race soever behave ill, they must be punished but not bribed."

The warrior's reaction was to hoard what little powder and ball he had and grumble about English stinginess. If the warrior did hunt, he then discovered that the general's policy had strictly limited the number of traders with whom he might do business. Amherst was hurting the Indian standard of living by these tactics; by others he was striking at the Indian's family ties. The tribesmen were most unwilling to surrender their captives. Many of them had been held for several years and had become adopted members of Indian families. A number of the women now had Indian children and were as reluctant to leave them as their husbands and adopted relatives were to see them go. Then the economy-minded English ceased supplying gifts to those Indians bringing in captives, a practice which had provided some compensation to the Indian for his loss. While the warriors digested this crowning indignity, they had to cope with an avalanche of English into the upper Ohio Valley as the French retreated. Pennsylvania had promised the Indians that they would not be disturbed west of the mountains, and the British commandant at Fort Pitt tried to hold back the waves of settlers by proclamation. As well might he have tried to reverse the flow of the Ohio.

Among the Delawares the Indians found hope of divine intervention. A prophet had arisen to preach a message that was to be preached many times among many tribes in the next century and a half. Like the Old Testament prophets the Delaware called for a return to the customs practiced before contamination by the invaders. Inspired by his message, which promised the removal of the whites if the tribesmen abandoned the use of firearms, blankets, and flint and steel, many Indians attempted to revert to a way of life the traders had so radically altered.

As the prophet's message spread beyond the bounds of the Delaware nation it was adapted to his own uses by Pontiac, an Ottawa warrior who twisted the prophet's words to aim only at the English and help convert Indian unrest into belligerency in the spring of 1763. That such an uprising was possible was apparent to Indian experts, but the outbreak, which was signaled by Pontiac's attack on Detroit in May, 1763, came as a complete surprise to Lord Amherst. As post after post fell, the one at Michilimackinac being infiltrated by warriors in the guise of lacrosse players, Amherst's shock turned to rage. He and his subordinate, Colonel Henry Bouquet, debated the respective merits of infecting the Indians with smallpox and hunting them with dogs. The proper breed of dogs was not available, but officers at Fort Pitt did distribute among the Delawares at least two handkerchiefs and two blankets from the smallpox hospital at the fort. Whether or not this early attempt at biological warfare was responsible, a smallpox epidemic was soon raging among the Delawares. If Amherst personally was not culpable, he certainly did not lament the Indian victims of the epidemic. He had made his sentiments clear in his letter to Bouquet in June, "I need only Add, that I Wish to Hear of *no Prisoners*, should any of the Villains be met with in Arms. . . ."

Although Pontiac failed at Detroit, within a short time it was the only post of nine west of Fort Pitt remaining in English hands. The Indian success was short-lived, for the uprising was confined to the Great Lakes frontier and lacked unity;

Pontiac had at best only a loose control over the tribesmen in the immediate vicinity of Detroit. By the end of the summer the whites had taken the initiative from the Indians and the uprising fell apart, but only after an estimated two thousand troops and settlers had been killed or captured. Like many a chief before and after him, Pontiac had found the individualism of the Indian an unsurmountable obstacle. One by one his allies came to terms with the English, Pontiac himself finally negotiating with Croghan. By 1765 quiet had descended once again on the northern frontier, not to be disturbed until Lord Dunmore's War of 1774.

Between 1763 and 1774 the English made and remade their Indian policy. More than two years before Pontiac took up the tomahawk, authorities in London were so disturbed by reports of Indian unrest that they reminded several of the colonial governments of the value of good Indian relations and forbade any further grants of lands claimed by Indians. By June, 1763, the king had been presented a plan providing for a restricted and orderly settlement of the lands conquered from the French. Before action could be taken, Pontiac and his allies attacked along a wide front, but after some minor revisions the plan was promulgated in October as the Proclamation of 1763. Its importance to the Indians lay in the line it drew approximately along the crest of the Appalachians beyond which settlement was temporarily forbidden.

Next, an elaborate program for the control of trade and Indian affairs was worked out. Trade with the Indians was to be rigidly controlled by a licensing system supervised by agents appointed to the principal tribes, but the governors, resenting the loss of power and revenues, refused to co-operate. By 1768 the British accepted the inevitable and returned the

Indian trade to the control of the colonial governors. The fate
of the land provisions was similar. Designed to reduce friction
between the races by erecting a barrier against white expansion, it proved totally inadequate. Squatters ignored it, and
colonial officials connived with speculators and promoters in
grandiose schemes involving Indian lands. The forces at work
were too dynamic to be contained by the machinery of the
British Empire. The crown was prepared to back down, but
the damage had been done. The Indians had been led to expect
protection which could not be provided and feeble gestures
in that direction had only alienated influential elements in the
colonies.

Two treaties negotiated to quiet the Indian title to land
immediately in the path of white settlements excited the Shawnees. They resented the English purchase from the Iroquois of
land the Shawnees claimed but were reassured that, for the
time being, the crown authorities did not intend to permit
settlement west of the Kanawha River. This would have safe-
guarded Shawnee hunting grounds, but the London authorities
did not allow for the insatiable Virginians. George Washington
and Patrick Henry were among the many busily dispatching
surveyors into Kentucky and lobbying for land grants in the
area presumably off limits to whites. When Governor Dunmore of Virginia was criticized for permitting such incendiary
activities he ruefully observed, ". . . they do and will remove
as their avidity and restlessness incite them. . . . Nor can they
be easily brought to entertain any belief of the permanent
obligation of Treaties made with those People, whom they
consider, as but little removed from the brute Creation."

By 1773 parties of surveyors had been fired upon in Kentucky, but the warnings went unheeded. Within a year Wheel-

ing and Pittsburgh were thronged with frontiersmen eager to beat the rush into the lands west of the Kanawha. Any hope that Pennsylvania authorities would restrain the whites before the Indians were provoked into war disappeared when Virginia laid claim to the forks of the Ohio. In the absence of any government prepared to defend Indian rights, frontiersmen in scattered incidents killed thirteen Indians, including relatives of Chief Logan. When he exacted an eye for an eye and a tooth for a tooth, Lord Dunmore called out the Virginia militia and the war was on.

In Lord Dunmore's War the Shawnees found themselves fighting virtually alone. Only enough of the Mingos, a western fragment of the Iroquois, joined the Shawnees to justify destruction of Mingo towns by the Virginia militia. Led by their chief, Cornstalk, who had worked to avoid the rupture until Dunmore called out the militia, the Shawnees unleashed but one real attack. Directed against a camp of Virginians at Point Pleasant at the mouth of the Kanawha, it ended in the Indian retreat across the Ohio after an all-day battle. Suing for peace on Virginia's terms, the Shawnees were taught a lesson in the futility of resistance which would keep them neutral in the early stages of the Revolution.

In the South the Cherokees had ample reason to assume the role played by the Shawnees in the North. The propensity of the Virginians for sharp tactics was revealed in the process of drawing a boundary line for a Cherokee cession. Surveyors confused two rivers and drew the lines of the cession to include more than the Cherokees had actually sold, but after the whites realized their error they failed to compensate the tribe. Theirs was a double standard of morality; one for dealing with white men, one for dealing with red men.

Colonial Preparation

Obviously, the plans of the crown for protection of Indian rights in land had broken down as completely as had their control of the fur trade. Traders' profits were declining as rapidly as the costs of administering Indian affairs were mounting. By 1775 Boston merchants were not alone in their dissatisfaction with the British conduct of affairs in North America. Philadelphia and Charleston houses with heavy financial commitments to the fur trade and the numerous land companies organized to exploit the lands won from France were equally unhappy. The attempt to shift some of the burden of imperial debt to the colonists did not appear as nearly so important a justification for revolution on the frontier as British policies on Indian land and trade.

By the time colonial discontent had paved the way for a new nation the pattern of white-Indian relations in what was to be the United States had already become apparent. Scores of Indian tribes, such as King Philip's Wampanoags, had been corrupted and eliminated by the whites. The outline of events in such tragedies was clear. The traders first employed the Indians to gather furs and tribal standard of living rose as they acquired firearms and metal tools. Then as the game diminished and the frontier line pressed upon the Indian holdings the second act opened. It closed with the tribesmen having been forced or seduced into selling their land. Occasionally this act would include an Indian war with a standard script calling for an outburst of violence by the tormented natives, scalpings, burning, and the horrors of torture embellished by that early American form of literature, the captivity narrative. The third act would find the Indian resistance crushed and the inevitable treaty written ceding even more land to the whites. The principal problem remaining would be the ultimate disposition of the tribe. The Indians might settle the problem temporarily by migrating westward to compete with already established tribes for their hunting grounds and set the stage for a repetition of the last two acts. Or, if the defeat in the war had been overwhelming, the few tribesmen remaining might be absorbed by neighboring bands or located on a reservation. The usual result was that the reservation Indians frustrated their well-wishers and co-operated with their oppressors by dying off rapidly.

The role of the central government, to be played by the United States after the Revolution, had already assumed definite character as portrayed by the British Empire. Basically paternal in their approach to Indian problems, officials of the central government soon learned that when a conflict existed between the interests of the Indians and those of the frontiersmen, that the Indians had to be sacrificed. To the extent that the Revolution would produce a new nation more responsive to its citizen's pressures, the Indians would lose by the change.

II

Foes and Friends, 1776-1816

Controversy over Indian trade and lands had helped precipitate the Revolution. The Declaration of Independence charged George III with trying to loose on the frontiersmen "the merciless Indian savages, whose known rule of warfare is an undistinguished destruction of all ages, sexes, and conditions." That most of the red men would remain loyal to the English was apparent immediately. The English could pose as defenders of Indian land against the avarice of the settlers, and the indispensable trade goods were available in the best quality and at the cheapest prices from English traders. Agents whom the Indians had come to trust worked to keep them loyal.

The Indians who supported the American cause were the exception. Some were influenced by traders who threw in their lot with the patriots and propagandized their Indian relatives and long-time customers. A few tribesmen listened to Congregational missionaries who used their positions of confidence and trust to counteract the Anglicans.

American Indians

Initially both the English and the Americans were reluctant to employ the Indians in military operations. Expensive and difficult to control, they waged a type of warfare which would defeat any hope of reconciliation, proponents of which were many in the early stages of the Revolution. But it was inevitable that the Indians should be drawn into the conflict, and the colonists were accused of employing them as early as the siege of Boston. The English justified their recruitment of Indian auxiliaries for the king's armies and dispatched messengers with ammunition to the Creeks and Cherokees. It was not difficult to arouse the Indians since they were already exasperated by the settlers' encroachments in the east Tennessee valleys. Led by Chief Dragging Canoe, the Cherokees launched attacks which not only failed but provoked crushing retaliatory action by the Americans. In 1777 the Cherokees were forced to sign treaties ceding large tracts of land.

The English found it very expensive to maintain the morale of the defeated Cherokees and at the same time keep the Creeks and Chickasaws in line. The king's agents also had to prevent the Choctaws from being corrupted by the Spanish agents among them. Muskets, powder and ball, knives, blankets, and handkerchiefs had to be distributed wholesale and prominent Indians such as Alexander McGillivray of the Creeks maintained on the payroll of the British army. Although the English grumbled and protested, they realized there was no alternative. Only in the area northwest of the Ohio River were they really dependent upon Indian aid; elsewhere their principal objective was to deny it to the Americans.

To the north the Iroquois might have been held loyal to the English cause had Sir William Johnson not died in 1774. Guy Johnson, his nephew and son-in-law, was unable to maintain the loyalty of the Oneidas and Tuscaroras, although a majority of the other four nations of the Iroquois did oppose the Americans. Skenandoa, an Oneida chief who had befriended the Congregationalist missionary Samuel Kirkland, helped ally his people with the Americans.

George III had a powerful friend in the Mohawk warrior Joseph Brant, the brother of Mary Brant, who presided over Sir William Johnson's household in Johnson's later years and bore him eight children. Taken under his wing by Johnson while Joseph was in his early teens, the fullblood Mohawk became one of the first of his tribe to read and write English. He also became a member of the Anglican church and served briefly as an interpreter for a missionary. When war came, he was serving as secretary to Guy Johnson and accompanied him to England, where Brant had tea with Boswell and sat for a portrait by Romney. Returning to America, he tried to whip up Iroquois enthusiasm for the war effort. The British success in driving Washington out of New York in 1776 encouraged the fence straddlers among the Iroquois to heed Brant's appeal, but the Iroquois were understandably reluctant to get involved in this unpleasantness. They had learned in the French and Indian War that fighting the white man's battles for him could be expensive.

North of the Ohio River the Indians were even less militant, and if the expedition Congress sent against Canada had retained its hold on the St. Lawrence the northern tribes would have been forced to deal with the Americans in order to get trade goods. But prodded by the English and encouraged by a deluge of gifts after the St. Lawrence was reopened, those Indians did launch a series of raids which harassed frontier settlements. The British commander in Canada directed that the war parties be intrusted to "proper persons," but the warriors were known to lift both Tory and Patriot scalps in their enthusiasm.

American opinion was that the most they could hope for was Indian neutrality, but even that would be a great help. Having been educated in the four wars with France the colonists gave the Indian problem high priority in their planning. The Provincial Congress of New York instructed its delegates in the Continental Congress to get some action on the Indian problem because:

our public peace is more endangered by the situation of the barbarians to the westward of us, than it can be by any inroads made upon the seacoast. Britain will spare the last for her own sake, and policy will teach her ministers to light upon an Indian war upon our frontier, that we may be drawn for protection to embrace the terms of slavery.

After the nomination of Washington as commander-in-chief, Congress did appoint a committee to examine the situation on the New York frontier and make recommendations. By July, 1775, the committee had reported and Congress established northern, middle, and southern departments to handle Indian affairs. People of the caliber of Patrick Henry served on the congressional committee examining the Indian question and acted as commissioners for the departments.

To the powerful Iroquois confederation Congress sent a message to be delivered in council by the northern commissioners. Seven hundred tribesmen of the Six Nations negotiated for a week with the Americans, drinking their rum and eating their rations, and meditating in their deliberate fashion on the advice of Congress to view this as a "family quarrel between us and Old England . . . and not join on either side, but keep the hatchet buried deep." A Mohawk sachem, Little Abraham, finally expressed the Indian determination to "sit still and see you fight it out." Unfortunately for the American cause the tribesmen present were only one faction of the Six Nations, and other Iroquois were even then in Montreal with Brant and Guy Johnson preparing to wage war against the Americans.

Congress was also concerned about the Delawares and stationed agents among them and subsidized the education of their youths at Dartmouth College and the College of New Jersey, Princeton's forerunner. Dartmouth even received grants for the education of young Canadian Indians in the hope that their attendance at the American school would contribute to the neutrality of their tribes. The Delawares were actually offered the prospect of statehood in a treaty negotiated in 1778. Fortunately, the willingness of the thirteen states to admit an Indian state to their ranks was not put to the test.

Just as the colonies had opposed the efforts of the crown to impose a unified Indian and land policy, so did the thirteen states resist the efforts of Congress under the Articles of Confederation to make policy in those areas. The extent to which the issue was compromised is explicit in the wording of the clause in the Articles which reserved for the Congress control of trade and tribal affairs of those Indians "not members of any of the states." Throughout the Revolution individual states impaired the American war effort by fighting and negotiating with tribes without consulting Congress.

As the Indians took a more active role in the war, the usual tactic of the frontiersmen was to erect stockades and remain on the defensive. This proved an invitation to disaster. Striking here and there according to no apparent pattern, war parties cut off families before they could retreat to the stockade and destroyed crops and livestock in the fields. Many of the pioneers gave up the struggle and abandoned their frontier farms.

In 1777 New York was the scene of the British effort to split the colonies by Burgoyne's wedge driven from Canada. Painted Indian warriors numbered about half of the force that tried to fight its way east along the Mohawk Valley to meet Burgoyne on the lower Hudson. The main force also included Indian auxiliaries, but not in the number promised Burgoyne. Unable to assure his victory, Burgoyne's Indians actually contributed to his defeat by a notorious incident. Warriors spearheading the British advance murdered Jenny McCrea, a young American girl trying to join her fiancé who was an officer serving with Burgoyne. In a letter to Burgoyne designed as propaganda, General Horatio Gates blasted the British commander for hiring "the savages of America to scalp Europeans and the descendants of Europeans, nay more, that he should pay a price for each scalp so barbarously taken. . . ." Gates's masterpiece circulated widely in New England and aided in turning out in record numbers the militia who helped force the surrender of Burgoyne.

The Americans frequently hurled the charge of scalp-buying against the British. Frenchmen were horrified by Franklin's fabrications which purported to prove the British were buying American hair by the bale. Kentucky frontiersmen were equally convinced Lieutenant-Governor Henry Hamilton was operating a scalp market at Detroit. The British had no set tariff on scalps, but they naturally regarded them as evidence of commendable activity and compensated their allies accordingly. Only to the extent that they had fewer Indian allies were the Americans themselves less guilty in this respect, despite Gates's letter to Burgoyne.

Foes and Friends, 1776–1816

Burgoyne's defeat had precipitated the French entrance into the war as an active ally of the Americans. Heretofore the Americans had tried to sway the Indians by references to secret French aid; now they employed French officers to visit tribes. Some Indians were impressed, but most held fast to their English Father. Their most devastating raids in the Mohawk and Wyoming valleys came in 1778 after the Franco-American alliance was signed. Washington and the Virginia authorities both concluded that some offensive strategy was in order, but they disagreed on objectives. Virginia wanted expeditions against Detroit and the Illinois country to eliminate the English influence responsible for the attacks on Kentucky. Washington gave Niagara the greater priority, since from it came many of the war parties that terrorized settlers on the Pennsylvania–New York frontier and destroyed the grain upon which his commissary was dependent. Therefore, unaided, Virginia undertook the offensive against the Illinois country and authorized George Rogers Clark, who had originally conceived the strategy, to carry it out. In a brilliant campaign Clark invaded the Illinois country and at least temporarily relieved pressure on the Virginia frontier by intimidating the tribesmen. To frighten an English garrison into surrendering, Clark's men resorted to psychological warfare and tomahawked four bound Indians in full view of the fort.

Such atrocities were not unknown in the campaigns of 1779 which Washington directed against the Indians who had been harassing Pennsylvania and New York. The principal thrust was General John Sullivan's against the hostile Iroquois towns. He blighted one of the most advanced Indian societies in North America. Scores of brick and stone homes were demolished, hundreds of acres of corn, beans, and melons were

destroyed, and orchards were girdled or cut down. Little resistance was encountered as the population of the towns retreated to the shelter of British posts, but not all escaped. Two
Indians killed were partially flayed to provide boot tops for
troops as addicted to souvenir-hunting as their twentieth-
century counterparts. The crusading zeal with which Sullivan's troops approached their task is reflected in a toast drunk
by his officers during the campaign, "Civilization or death to
all American savages."

Sullivan's raid may have taught some of the tribesmen the
futility of resistance, but it only antagonized others. In the
last two years of the war the Indians were on the offensive in
the North. In the South, Choctaws joined the garrison of
Savannah in defending it against American attacks, and Creeks
attacked the besiegers from without. In view of their apparent
successes, the Indians' shock at the terms ending the war is
understandable. Despite their sacrifices for the common cause,
no provision was made for them in the treaty. The British
granted the Americans title to the entire Northwest, disregarding the occupying tribesmen who had had the Americans
on the defensive when the war ended.

Angry and confused, the Indians were reluctant to negotiate with the Americans. Joseph Brant spoke for the
Iroquois and flatly declined to conclude hostilities until the
United States recognized the land claims of the Six Nations.
North of the Ohio the new government was asserting title to
Indian lands as far west as the Miami and Maumee on the
grounds that the tribes of that area had forfeited their title by
aiding the English. In the South the Indian position was worsened by complete dependence now upon either the Spanish

in Florida and Louisiana or the Americans in Georgia and the Carolinas for the vital trade goods.

The atmosphere in the mid-1780's was not conducive to peace. Racial animosities had been aggravated by the war and as late as three years after the Revolution, Congress was still negotiating the release of prisoners. The settlers and land speculators regarded the end of the fighting as they had regarded the end of the French and Indian War, as a signal to move the frontier line deeper into Indian country. One frontiersman argued that "all mankind . . . have an undoubted right to pass into every vacant country, and a spokesman for western Pennsylvania denied that "the animals vulgarly called the Indians" had any natural rights in the land.

This line of reasoning was apparent in the actions of states with Indian populations. Georgia and North Carolina took the Articles of Confederation at face value and negotiated dubious treaties or by legislative action took over Indian lands. The state governments, harsh as their tactics may seem, were accurately reflecting the desires of enfranchised Georgians and Carolinians. They were already employing the rationalization used extensively to justify white aggression: God and reason both condemn the monopoly of land by those unprepared to cultivate it.

Congress did inherit from the British government both a claim to jurisdiction over Indian affairs and a responsibility for protecting Indian rights. In 1783 it issued a proclamation warning against purchases of or squatting on Indian lands. Two years later Congress ordered frontiersmen to stay south of the Ohio and when the order was ignored troops were used, as they had been around Fort Pitt in 1762, to burn cabins

39

and evict squatters. The result was much the same. The whites could not be restrained and the Indians retaliated by lifting sundry scalps. The whites replied by filibustering expeditions which, as was the case with the Indian war parties also, frequently punished the innocent. Both Indians and whites simply bypassed the inadequate forces Congress stationed along the disputed frontier.

The weakness of the Articles of Confederation was nowhere more apparent than in its feeble efforts to cope with the Indian problem. Apparently barred by the language of the Articles from infringing upon a state's right to abuse Indians resident within its boundaries, Congress was equally futile in dealing with the Indians beyond state boundaries. A clause in a treaty in 1785 permitting the Cherokees to send a representative to Congress was as unrealistic as the earlier proposal for an Indian state. The frontiersman was not interested in a paternal policy which would civilize the Indian if it meant safeguarding the aborigine's land and property. The last thing the frontiersman was prepared to countenance was the creation of an Indian state and Indian representation in Congress. Illustrative of the atmosphere on the frontier was an army officer's comment that, "The people of Kentucky will carry on private expeditions against the Indians and kill them whenever they meet them, and I do not believe that there is a jury in all Kentucky who would punish a man for it."

After 1783 the natural rivalry was heightened by the role played by the English in the North and the Spanish in the South. Concern for the fur trade and a possible resumption of hostilities conditioned the actions of Englishmen. Fur traders operating out of Canada encouraged the Indians to confederate and hold out for the Ohio River as a boundary. As early as

1783 the governor of Quebec suggested to superiors in London that the area between the Ohio River and Canada be reserved to the Indians. This concept of a barrier state was to complicate the negotiations concluding the War of 1812. For the present it was not pushed, but the English did retain several forts on American soil, the notorious Northwest Posts. From these, English traders and officials did not dispatch raiders against the American settlers, as Americans claimed, but they obviously did work to keep the Indians friendly to England and aware of American misconduct. This inspired among the red men the persistent belief that they could depend upon the English when the chips were down.

Farther south the Indians were turning to the Spanish for support in the face of steady pressure from American speculators and settlers. Their most able leader was the Creek mixed blood, Alexander McGillivray. He did not correspond to the popular impression of an Indian leader. Not a dashing warrior, McGillivray depended upon cool bargaining to beat the whites at their own game. Nor did he overawe his fellow tribesmen by his recital of feats of bravery on the warpath; he kept the Creek towns in line by threatening to deprive them of their white traders. In the decade after the Revolution, McGillivray helped the Creeks maintain a united front and played off Spain and the United States against each other. Although this educated Indian was more at home in a drawing room than on a battlefield, he was not averse to his subordinates leading war parties. Beginning in 1786, Creek warriors struck at settlements along the Georgia frontier and frightened the Spanish with the prospect of being drawn into a war with the United States.

There was more skirmishing along the Ohio also in 1786.

Small parties of warriors and frontiersmen carried on a nasty warfare which did not produce many casualties in any one engagement but kept nerves on edge and made neutrality difficult for both Indians and Americans. Joseph Brant tried to persuade the tribes to confederate for effective opposition to the Americans and went to England to seek assistance. As the situation along the frontier deteriorated, Congress rebuked Virginia for permitting whites to provoke an Indian war. Congress also proceeded to reorganize its Indian service and bring the fur trade under closer surveillance.

Had these steps been taken earlier, perhaps some of the friction on the frontier could have been avoided, but perhaps not. The conflict between the principle and practice can be seen in the phrasing of the Ordinance of 1787 and the instructions given the governor of the Northwest Territory. The Ordinance provided the framework of government for the Northwest and specified:

The utmost good faith shall always be observed towards the Indians; their lands and property shall never be taken from them without their consent; and in their property, rights and liberty, they shall never be invaded or disturbed, unless in just and lawful wars authorized by Congress. . .

Fine words, but some of Governor Arthur St. Clair's earliest instructions were not to "neglect any opportunity . . . of extinguishing the Indian rights to the westward as far as the River Mississippi" and to adhere to treaties already drafted "unless a change of boundary, beneficial to the United States can be obtained." Congress was encountering the same difficulty as the crown in serving the interests of the settlers and at the same time protecting Indian rights.

The framers of the Constitution had less to say on the

Indian issue than did those who wrote the Articles of Confederation. Indians were mentioned only in connection with Congress' control of commerce. In this, as in so many things, it was the precedents established in the early years which determined the tenor of federal Indian policy. Washington and his advisers were in agreement on reserving for the federal government even greater authority in this field than Congress had wielded under the Articles.

Henry Knox continued to serve as Secretary of War and administer Indian policy as he had in the last years of the Articles. The Secretary had strong views on the subject that he did not hesitate to expound to Washington. While the incidents multiplied along the frontier, Knox was prepared to hold both whites and Indians responsible and urged measures to restrain the settlers and civilize the Indians. The process would be neither cheap nor easy, but it would certainly be preferable to wars of extermination, and Knox was sensitive that our English-American policies had been more destructive to the natives than policies pursued in Mexico and Peru.

The Secretary was one of the first public officials to emphasize private property as an instrument of civilization. Following the Lockean line which was to become so popular in the next century and ultimately produce the Dawes Severalty Act, Knox argued that if ownership in fee simple were introduced among the tribesmen they would be stimulated to acquire the white man's techniques in order to enhance the value of their property. Missionaries resident among the Indian nations could further the good work by introducing their neophytes to the implements and the domestic animals which lightened the farmer's chores and raised his standard of living. Knox assumed that the tribes would be removed or, pos-

American Indians

sibly, absorbed. He envisioned the pioneers invading Indian hunting grounds and, by killing the game upon which the red men depended, conditioning them to sell their lands and move farther West. But how was this continued retreat to be reconciled with the program to civilize the Indians by locating them on their own farms? Knox was one of the first officials to face this dilemma. With the best of intentions, he could not reserve for the Indians the land necessary for their civilization because enfranchised frontiersmen had priority. The early 1790's was no more propitious for such a program than the 1690's had been or the 1890's were to be. Regardless of the century, the reactions of a frontiersman to the sight of good arable land in the possession of an Indian were as easy to predict as the reflexes of Pavlov's dog.

Feeling their way gradually in the face of the secession threats of Kentuckians and Tennesseans, Washington's and Adams' administrations formulated policy. Between 1790 and 1799 four temporary trade and intercourse acts were passed. They provided that trade with the Indians was to be limited to those holding government licenses and that these licenses might be canceled for failure to abide by regulations. Indian lands might be purchased only at public treaties sponsored by the United States, and squatters and illegal surveyors might be removed by military force. Thus, the federal government had established itself as a protector of the Indian's rights in land against any third party. However, the effect of this was weakened in 1799 by orders to the military to handle squatters "with all the humanity which the circumstances will possibly permit." For army officers in a civilian-dominated military establishment this was sufficient warning. If Indian and white interests conflicted, the Indian was sacrificed. This was also

44

apparent in the history of the government stores, or factories.

The "factory" system was an interesting attempt to make available to the Indians trade goods at cost, thus combating English and Spanish influence among the tribes. Inaugurated in 1795, the first two stores were located among the Creeks and Cherokees whose trade had been virtually monopolized by an English firm McGillivray had persuaded the Spanish to sponsor. These factories and their approximately twenty companion ventures which developed under the general law of 1796 were not as effective as had been hoped. But neither were they the failures described by their opponents. The factors in charge, despite their instructions to restrict credit and the requirement that they sell only American products, which were frequently inferior to the English equivalents, did help counteract the machinations of foreign agents and pave the way for other American policies.

Washington referred repeatedly to these policies in his talks to delegations of Indians. The President advised the tribesmen to adopt the white man's farming and stock-raising methods. Agents among the tribes did the same, but the appropriations to encourage these changes were too small to be effective. Beginning in 1793 Congress authorized an expenditure of no more than $20,000 annually for the purchase of domestic animals and farming implements for the Indian nations. It is doubtful if much of this was expended for purely civilizing projects. Federal agents apparently drew on this fund for the gifts needed to influence important tribal leaders and to entertain tribal delegations.

But even the best of policies were worthless unless proper personnel were available to implement them. The quality of the early agents seems to have been high, but they were certainly not numerous, only about twenty-five as late as the War of 1812. Governors of the territories also acted as ex officio superintendents for their territories, but confusion arose when the governor reported to the Secretary of State in his capacity as governor, and to the Secretary of War in his capacity as superintendent of Indian affairs for the territory. An additional difficulty lay in the jurisdictional disputes between civilians and the military when the army had to be brought in to cope with hostile Indians. In the century after 1789 this was frequent.

The Indians south of the Ohio were slow to respond to the American agents and the policies they hoped to implement. While the Constitution was being framed in Philadelphia, Creek warriors were on the warpath, armed if not encouraged by the Spanish then occupying both Florida and Louisiana. The Cherokees were only relatively less hostile, and only the Chickasaw and the Choctaw nations, free of settler pressure, could be said to have been friendly.

Among the Creeks McGillivray was the guiding force until his death in 1793. Subsidized by the Spanish his last four years, for at least part of that time he was also receiving an annuity from the United States. Yet the man cannot be dismissed summarily as a creature prepared to sell his people for gold. While both the Americans and Spanish thought that they had bribed him, his unusual talents were dedicated to maintaining Creek interests regardless of whose payroll he might be on at the moment.

In the late 1780's McGillivray was thinking of a confederation of southern tribes comparable to that struggling for definition north of the Ohio. Backed by the Spanish, they might be able to withstand the pressure of the Georgians who wanted to clear their state of the Creeks. Like many others, Mc-Gillivray did not have much respect for the prowess of the United States, with which the Creeks had not yet signed a treaty. Indeed, until the Territory South of the River Ohio was created in early 1790 the federal government had had little contact with the southern tribes. An attempt to negotiate with the Creeks had failed in 1789, but the following year McGillivray journeyed to New York accompanied by an elaborate retinue, establishing a precedent for junkets to the capital by tribal delegations. Wined and dined, McGillivray consented to sign the Treaty of New York establishing relations with the United States. By secret clauses he accepted the honorary rank of brigadier general and an annuity of $1,200. The United States seems to have derived very little from the bribes given McGillivray and his subordinates, and Georgians were enraged that the treaty recognized Creek claims in their state.

If nothing else, the treaty motivated the Spanish to be more generous with McGillivray and his fellow tribesmen. Nevertheless, the chief and his people were not happy. The Georgians, whom the Creeks dubbed "People-greedily-grasping-after-land," were relentless in their pressure, and the federal government, despite Knox's assurances at New York, was not an effective counterforce. Nor were the Spanish the bulwark McGillivray had hoped for; their enthusiasm ebbed and flowed. Little wonder that the ablest diplomat the Indians have produced described his mood shortly before his death as "approaching to a despondency."

No Creek was of sufficient stature to replace McGillivray whose passing London journals recorded in space normally reserved for death notices of English lords. The man Washington appointed in 1796 as Creek agent and superintendent of southern Indians did come to enjoy considerable influence among the tribesmen. Acquainted with the Creeks and Creek problems for a decade, Benjamin Hawkins had represented North Carolina in the Senate one term before he disregarded the advice of friends and family and with missionary zeal devoted the remaining twenty years of his life to the Creeks. Until the War of 1812, Hawkins succeeded in keeping the tribe at peace with the whites in spite of the provocative acts of the settlers who grazed their cattle on the Indian's land and slaughtered the game upon which his family depended. In the face of official hypocrisy and Indian apathy the agent tried to convert his charges to agriculture, preaching the virtues of fencing and private property and using his own plantation as a model farm.

Agent Hawkins had many occasions to doubt the efficacy of any plan to civilize the Indians. Georgia in the 1790's sold to speculators over twenty-five million acres of tribal lands, an action indicative of the state's unwillingness to permit the Indians to remain, civilized or not. Many Creeks discouraged their children from frequenting the few schools available, believing that educated Indians "turned out very worthless: became mischievous and troublesome, and involve the red and white people in difficulties." Hawkins did make some converts, especially among the half-bloods. By 1800 communal ownership was still the pattern, but here and there a tribesman had appropriated tribal land for his individual use and was adopting the farming methods of his white contemporaries. Some had become so civilized as to own Negro slaves.

There was also evidence of change among the Cherokees,

the other prominent southern tribe in contact with Americans between 1789 and 1800. The Cherokees were emboldened by their Spanish connection and were also exposed to British propaganda. Some Cherokee bands had moved north of the Ohio River after the Revolution, and through them the British maintained a tenuous contact with the southern Indians. The connection might have been more significant had the Spanish and McGillivray not opposed it. Certainly the Indian successes in the North against American troops under Harmar and St. Clair encouraged leaders like old Dragging Canoe to conspire, independently of McGillivray, for a confederation of southern Indians. The elderly Cherokee chief dreamed of a return to 1777, when he and his warriors had terrorized Kentucky. But in the fifteen years that elapsed Americans had swarmed to the frontier and the Cherokee population had declined. In the early 1790's there was no concerted Cherokee effort to evict the squatters on their lands, but here and there white men were killed. Expeditions of Tennessee frontiersmen, coupled with Anthony Wayne's victory in the North and the Spanish retreat by the Treaty of San Lorenzo, convinced the Cherokees that resistance was futile. By 1800 there was evidence in the tribe that civilization had made a little headway, although among the lower Cherokees in central Georgia the society of the hunter still persisted. One band migrated west of the Mississippi, as the game disappeared from their hunting grounds in Georgia, to avoid farming.

North of the Ohio River the tribes had not been impressed by the inauguration of the Constitution, nor did the settlers stop intruding on Indian land. Instead, the frontiersmen expected the new federal government to provide them the backing they had lacked under the Articles of Confederation. One estimate was that 1,500 Kentuckians lost their lives as a result of Indian action between 1783 and 1790.

Negotiation could not produce peace as long as treaties were simply means of securing more Indian land. Three of them had been negotiated with the Ohio Indians between 1785 and 1789, but in one instance an important tribe was not represented and at the last conference the Americans had their way only because of divisions among the tribesmen. Some of the Indians wanted to stand by the Ohio River boundary, others argued that this was already lost and the line should be drawn farther west.

In 1789, General Josiah Harmar commanded the American forces north of the Ohio and was impatient to solve the problem by a punitive expedition into the Indian country. He even hinted that the Kentucky freebooters had his approval. Governor Arthur St. Clair likewise felt the faction-ridden Indian confederation ripe for attack. These internal differences he was "not willing to lessen"; he was prepared to use them to set the Indians "at deadly variance," recalling the earlier tactic of setting the wolf packs against each other.

At the head of a motley array, mostly militia with a stiffening of regulars who themselves were poorly equipped and ill trained, Harmar was given his chance to settle the Indian problem in the fall of 1790. In three skirmishes that followed, the Miamis' Little Turtle and the Shawnees' Blue Jacket inflicted over two hundred casualties on the ragged army and desertion weakened the force still further. About five weeks after the campaign began, Harmar's force was back at its point of departure having done little more than raise Indian morale.

Smithsonian Institution

Cheyenne horse travois (photograph by Christian Barthelmess, about 189?).

Chippewa hunters (photograph by Roland Reed, about 1900)

Smithsonian Institution

Pawnee earth lodge village, 1871 (photograph by William H. Jackson)

Navaho woman at loom, 1880 (photograph by Wittick)

St. Clair's turn was next. The governor was commissioned major general for the occasion and in October, 1791, led a larger force north. He was plagued with the same absence of discipline and training, and shortages in equipment. Attacked one dawn while encamped on the Maumee River, St. Clair's army dissolved in panic and fled south after suffering over nine hundred casualties in one of the worst defeats ever inflicted by the Indians on a white army.

The effect of these two victories was to strengthen the hand of the warriors insisting on the Ohio River as the boundary and to inspire previously unenthusiastic tribes like the Delawares and Wyandots. English officials in Canada added fuel to the flames by predicting that the negotiations between John Jay and British diplomats would break down. The warriors who had defeated Harmar and St. Clair were in no mood to buy peace. It took another expedition to make them more cooperative.

This time the tribesmen had to contend with General Wayne. He belied his nickname of "Mad Anthony" by methodical planning which produced a disciplined, trained, and equipped force which even included a few Chickasaw and Choctaw scouts. As the Indians confidently gathered to resist this latest invasion, instructions were en route from London to Canada to prepare officials there for the pending evacuation of the Northwest Posts in anticipation of the signing of the Jay Treaty.

Ignorant of the ways of white diplomats and assuming that the English could be counted upon if the occasion demanded, 2,000 Shawnees, Miamis, and other tribesmen from the Old Northwest, plus some Creeks and Cherokees and a number of Canadian traders, prepared to annihilate the Americans. When the cautious Wayne failed to bring on a battle immediately, the impatient warriors began to lose interest and return to their villages. Trying to keep his force intact, Little Turtle launched an assault against Fort Recovery, garrisoned by a small detachment of Wayne's army. Beaten off, Little Turtle lost even more warriors as they became discouraged and headed for home. When Wayne launched the Battle of Fallen Timbers in August, 1794, only 1,300 of the original force of 2,000 Indians were in the vicinity and possibly as many as 500 of these were begging food from the British post four miles away. The warriors did not suffer many casualties, but their lines were broken and the English were unwilling to challenge Wayne. The Indians had to stand by helplessly and watch the Americans burn villages and destroy the stands of corn the general described as larger than any he had ever before seen. Although small bands of diehards continued to harass American outposts and cut off foraging parties, the Indian will to resist had been broken.

As winter approached, hungry and tattered Indian delegations called on Wayne and asked for peace. Formal negotiations did not get under way until June, 1795, but by August the Treaty of Greenville was ready for signature. The Indians accepted small annuities and ceded to the United States most of the present state of Ohio, a small area in Indiana, and enclaves elsewhere for American posts. Deserted by the English who had already withdrawn from the Northwest Posts, the red men's position was bitterly summed up by Joseph Brant, "This is the second time the poor Indians have been left in the lurch."

Although Brant had been very active immediately following the Revolution in the attempts to form a confederation to block American expansion, the Iroquois did not figure in the three campaigns which culminated in the Battle of Fallen Timbers. Following 1783 most of the Mohawks and Cayugas and portions of the other Six Nations moved west of the Niagara River and accepted reservations from the English. Those Iroquois who remained in New York showed some interest in civilization; the Senecas asked for schools for their children and instruction in vocational subjects for their adults. The government was too preoccupied with the hostile Indians northwest of the Ohio to expend much time or money educating the dispirited remnants of a once proud and fearless people. As Seneca chiefs like Cornplanter and Red Jacket debated the merits of a pro-English versus a pro-American policy, the people of the tribes succumbed to the vices represented equally well by either set of white men.

In the depths of their despair the Senecas produced a messiah. The elderly and dissipated Handsome Lake reported visions which became the basis for a new religion, one still practiced on Iroquois reservations in New York and Canada. The messiah's message stressed temperance, acculturation, the nuclear family, and the necessity of the Indians retaining their land. The Senecas were not asked to totally reject the old, just to modify it.

Comparable conditions among the Indians of the Old Northwest produced the movement associated with Tecumseh and his brother, Tenskwatawa, the Shawnee Prophet. Policies pursued under Thomas Jefferson and James Madison contributed to their rise. Despite their frequently proclaimed devotion to human rights, it was obvious that the two Virginians were not color blind when the inevitable conflicts between settlers and Indians arose. Jefferson, especially, lectured visiting delegations on the benefits of the American way of life, but he was prepared to remove Indians from their primitive farms in order to make way for white settlers. Jefferson could argue that any program of civilization to be successful required that the red men be isolated from the contaminating influence of the dissolute characters who thronged the frontier. However, Jefferson's vision of the government factories as a means of saddling influential Indians with heavy debt, thereby making them "willing to lop them off by a cession of lands," suggests the sort of duplicity Hamilton saw in his personality.

Jefferson was under severe pressure to satisfy the land hunger of frontiersmen still not immune to talk of the advantages of secession. The problem Georgia presented was especially thorny. Georgians had rebelled in righteous wrath over the sale of 20,000,000 acres to the Yazoo companies. However, John Marshall's Supreme Court upheld the validity of the original contracts. The compromise worked out in 1802 included an agreement that the United States would extinguish the Indian title to land in Georgia "as early as the same can be peaceably obtained, on reasonable terms." In this provision lay the seeds of trouble for all concerned. Although the compact did not specify that the Indians had to be removed from Georgia, it is obvious that this is what the Georgians read into it. The failure of the federal government to accomplish it as rapidly as they had hoped strengthened the state rights faction in Georgia politics. For the Indians involved, the compact was a disaster because it made a farce of any policy designed to civilize them in their homeland. Within a year Jefferson was formulating plans to move the Indians west of the Mississippi.

In the face of an impending French occupation of New Orleans Jefferson in February, 1803, instructed Governor

William Henry Harrison of Indiana Territory to negotiate land purchases from the Indians before French influence made them more difficult. The American purchase of Louisiana removed this threat, but the Indians continued to be pressed for cessions because Jefferson saw in the territory the answer to the Indian problem: they could be persuaded to exchange their lands east of the Mississippi for lands west of the river. As Jefferson explained it to a Chickasaw delegation in 1805, they should cease to depend on hunting, as their country was being stripped of game, and exchange their holdings in the East for land "unoccupied by any red men."

Jefferson first broached the subject of removal to Congress in 1803. Persisting, the President got written into the act organizing Louisiana Territory in 1804 a provision for an exchange of Indian lands and the drive got under way. Grudgingly, the tribesmen began to sell, but here and there persuasion was necessary. In 1808 when some of the Cherokees who had begun to acquire the benefits of civilization expressed a preference for severalty and citizenship without removal, Jefferson insisted on removal. By 1811, 2,000 Cherokees had migrated to the Arkansas country, but without ceding their land. President Madison declined a suggestion that the United States dictate terms, but what was done frequently made as much of a mockery of the treaty process. Tribes whose members had committed depredations along the frontier discovered that the easiest way to expiate their sins was by a land cession. Numerous treaties recorded in this period listed land grants, salaries, and other perquisites for those influential chiefs and half-bloods willing to co-operate in cessions. Silver medals, officers' coats and swords, and alcoholic refreshments helped condition tribal leaders. If the real leaders were not complaisant, then more plastic personalities were singled out for United States favor. Not unknown was the "delayed purchase" by which title to the land passed to the United States, but the Indians were not required to move until the line of settlement reached them, perhaps a quarter-century later. Then it would come as quite a shock to tribesmen, who had only the vaguest notion of ceding land by treaty, to learn that their villages and hunting grounds had been sold.

The most talented American at separating the Indians from their ancestral lands was undoubtedly William Henry Harrison, who served as governor of Indiana Territory, 1800–1812. During that period he was the prime mover in fifteen treaties which quieted tribal title to most of what is today Indiana and Illinois, a segment of Ohio, and smaller portions of Michigan and Wisconsin, at bargain prices which seldom ran over a cent an acre. Unhampered by scruples in dealing with the unsophisticated red men, on one occasion Harrison told a delegation slow to negotiate a cession that the United States could and would take the lands by force if the Indians did not sell. Down to 1811 violence was not required and everything was done legally, if not ethically.

The tactics of Harrison and his colleagues did inspire formidable opposition in the brother team, Tecumseh and the Shawnee Prophet. Tecumseh was the organizer, a man with a breadth of vision rare among Indians. He belonged to that handful of chiefs like King Philip, Pontiac, and Joseph Brant who recognized that only by forgetting their intertribal rivalries and animosities could the Indians even hope to stem the American advance. For his part, the Prophet supplied the spiritual re-enforcements and a mastery of the elements which enabled him to still the winds and stop the stars in their courses.

Tecumseh was also talented in this area. Legend has it that he could stamp his foot in his village on the Wabash and the reverberations would be felt by the Indians south of the Ohio.

The Shawnee brothers brought a messianic message which may have been just a revival of the doctrine of the Delaware Prophet. In addition to the summons to revert to original tribal purity, they also preached that individual tribes could not alienate land which was held in common by all the Indians of a region. As the message of the Shawnees converted tribesmen, Harrison found the task of purchasing land more difficult.

The governor's last major purchase was that consummated by the Treaty of Fort Wayne in 1809, when 2,500,000 acres changed hands. Tecumseh vainly protested this treaty to the governor, who described him as inspiring "implicit obedience and respect" in his followers. Reports flowed to Washington from the frontier telling of the Shawnee brothers' visits to tribes as far removed as the Cherokees, Choctaws, and Creeks in the South and the Sacs and the Sioux along the upper Mississippi. Harrison confided to the Secretary of War that were it not for the United States the Shawnee chief might create an empire "that would rival in glory Mexico or Peru."

Tecumseh did not seek war, nor did the British. But Tecumseh's objectives, short of divine intervention, could be achieved only by war, and the British had to indulge him the hope of British assistance. The king's agents were at their usual game, encouraging Indians to visit them, listening sympathetically to their complaints against the Americans, and inspiring the hope that someday the red coats would join the red men in driving the Americans back from the Ohio. As the United States and Great Britain teetered on the brink of war from 1807 to 1812 the king's agents could pursue no other policy. At any time they might need the services of their Indian allies. As early as 1806, Jefferson proposed that government trading posts in competition with Canadian traders operate at a loss if that were the only way to meet this threat.

To no one's surprise, hostilities finally erupted in the Old Northwest in the fall of 1811. After another vain protest against the Treaty of Fort Wayne, Tecumseh had informed Harrison that he was going to visit the southern tribes. The governor concluded that a preventive war was in order and in Tecumseh's absence marched troops into the heart of the Indian country. While the army was encamped near Prophet's Town at the mouth of Tippecanoe Creek, the threatened tribesmen struck the first blow. Swarming out of the village the brothers had made a haven for discontented elements of many tribes, the warriors led by the Prophet assaulted the American lines in clear violation of Tecumseh's orders. They were repulsed, and Prophet's Town was burned. When Tecumseh returned from the South, he no longer attempted to restrain his followers, and a frontier war was under way which merged in June with the War of 1812.

Historians still debate the specific weight to be assigned Indian affairs in America's decision to declare war on England in 1812. The actions of small bands of Winnebagos, Shawnees, and Potawatomis, supposedly supplied and inspired by the English, had had the frontier in turmoil for several years. The solution was summed up in one phrase by the West's representatives in Congress: "On to Canada!"

The war was the last in which the Indians were able to ally themselves with a foreign power against the United States. As usual there was no semblance of unity. In the South only the Creeks were in arms against the Americans and only a portion of that nation. In the Old Northwest the tribes were generally hostile, but even there probably not a single tribe could be found in which one or more bands were not neutral, if not pro-American. As auxiliaries for British forces the Indians had a certain nuisance value, but the day was gone when warriors constituted the balance of power.

South of the Ohio the Indian operations might be accurately described as a civil war. Tecumseh's reactionary ideas had found a warm reception among the Creek conservatives who resented Hawkins' vigorous program for civilization. The progressives not only championed the cultural innovations but, prodded by Hawkins, also condoned the sharp American tactics for securing cessions. The precipitating incident was the murder near the mouth of the Ohio, under the mistaken impression that war had been declared, of several white families by Creeks returning from a conference with the Shawnees. Hawkins insisted that the progressive-controlled tribal government punish the guilty, because the Tennesseans were threatening to hold the whole Creek nation responsible. When several of the culprits were killed resisting arrest the conservatives exacted revenge. Encouraged by their prophets who promised divine intervention the Red Sticks, as the belligerents were designated from their practice of carrying small painted wands of reputed mystic powers, attacked and destroyed towns of the progressives. Strongest among the upper Creeks, the Red Sticks dramatized their anti-civilization views by slaughtering the livestock of the progressives and wrecking mills, looms, and other symbols of the hated way of life. When they ran out of targets, they launched an attack against Fort

Mims on the lower Alabama River and massacred not only some of the despised progressives who had taken shelter there but also several hundred whites.

This incident gave credence to the charge that the Red Sticks were armed and inspired by British agents in Florida and provided the justification for an American campaign against the Indians. Under no circumstances could the Creek War be considered a conflict between the Creek Nation or the Southern Indians and the United States. A majority of the Creek warriors served in the army of Andrew Jackson, and Cherokees and Choctaws also fought the Red Sticks despite the presence in their tribes of vigorous conservative factions.

William McIntosh, a half-blood, led the Creek regiment supporting Jackson's campaign, and John Ross, who has been described as "a Scotchman with a dash of Cherokee blood," was conspicuous among the Cherokee companies. There were some glaring exceptions, however, to the rule that the mixed-bloods were usually found in the ranks of the progressives. William Weatherford, a nephew of Alexander McGillivray and at least half white, led the assault on Fort Mims. As Red Eagle, he was one of the principal Creek commanders when Jackson crushed the Red Sticks at the Battle of Horseshoe Bend. Contrariwise, Pushmataha, the Choctaw chief and a full-blood, threw his influence against Tecumseh when he visited the southern tribes in 1811 and helped align his people against the Red Sticks in the Creek War.

In August, 1814, five months after Jackson with the aid of his Indian allies had captured the Red Stick stronghold, the general dictated the Treaty of Fort Jackson. The terms fell heavily on all Creeks, whether Red Sticks or pro-American. Although they could hardly be said to have been participants in the War of 1812, the Creeks were the poorer as a result of it. Urged on by the frontiersmen, Jackson required the cession of nearly all the Creek lands in Alabama and a strip in Georgia along the Florida boundary. This separated the Creeks from their relatives the Seminoles and from the Spanish, Chickasaws, and Choctaws. The Georgians were badly disappointed that the opportunity was not taken to expel all the Creeks from their state and held Hawkins responsible for the failure. The agent, deeply regretting the harshness of the dictated settlement and the fatal schism his policies had produced among a people he loved, shortly resigned his position.

After the treaty negotiations, Jackson further demonstrated Indian gullibility by recruiting about a thousand Creek and Choctaw warriors for his push against the Florida tribes. The Indian capacity for self-destruction seemed limitless.

In the upper Mississippi Valley the Indians were much more united in their support of the British. In part this was due to their dependence on Canadian traders whose propaganda American agents were hard put to overcome. In Washington in August, 1812, in a talk to Indians from the upper Mississippi, President Madison made the American policy clear. He attributed the war to the king's attempt to make the "eighteen fires" "dig and plant for his people beyond the great water," and criticized the "bad birds" from Canada who were "sent out with bloody belts in their bills" to agitate the Indians. "And I say to you, my children, your father does not ask you to join his warrior," stated the President. "Sit still on your seats and be witnesses that they are able to beat their enemies, and protect their red friends."

The Americans did try, with little success, to relocate some of the tribes along the Missouri to keep them from contact with British agents. Despite Madison's statement, the Americans were happy to employ warriors where it was feasible. Lewis Cass and William Henry Harrison recruited fighting men from friendly tribes at a fixed rate of 60 cents a day for mounted warriors and $1.00 a day for chiefs. At St. Louis, Superintendent of Indian Affairs William Clark subsidized war parties of Pawnees, Osages, and Sioux to attack pro-British tribes and take the pressure off the frontier.

The British made no pretense of cultivating Indian neutrality. Six months before the declaration of war in June, 1812, their agents were submitting estimates of the warriors who would be available. The British advised the Indians to insist that the Americans retreat east of the line provided in 1795 by the Treaty of Greenville. But, as one agent was cautioned, "it is to be clearly understood that the Indians only are to appear as the movers in such proceedings." Posing as usual as defenders of Indian rights, the king's agents were generally successful in their contests with the Americans for tribal favor.

Indian auxiliaries were present at all British operations in the Old Northwest. They witnessed the surrender of Mackinac, and at Fort Dearborn got out of hand and massacred American prisoners. Tecumseh, as brigadier general in the British forces, was active in the engagements around Detroit. Without him the warriors would have been even more inclined to view the war as a series of raids with lengthy intermissions. Black Hawk, the Sac war chief, summed up the Indian view of white tactics when he remarked disgustedly, "Instead of stealing upon each other, and taking every advantage to *kill the enemy* and *save their own people*, as we do . . . they march out in open daylight, and *fight* regardless of the number of warriors they may lose!"

The initiative around Detroit lay with Tecumseh and his British allies until the Americans went on the offensive in the summer of 1813. Outnumbered and intimidated, the British general retreated, despite Tecumseh's scornful demand that, if he did not intend to fight, he turn over his equipment to the Indians. "We are determined to defend our lands, and if it be his [the Great Spirit's] will, we wish to leave our bones upon them," vowed the Shawnee. Finally forced to stand and fight at the Battle of the Thames, the British were badly defeated by the Americans under William Henry Harrison, and Tecumseh was killed. There were several claimants to the honor of having slain Tecumseh. One report was that he was flayed and his skin made into souvenir razor straps by the representatives of the higher way of life.

Farther west the tribesmen were more successful. Throughout the war raiding parties of pro-British warriors menaced settlements as far south as St. Louis. The American scheme to plant a garrison at Prairie du Chien to command the Mississippi above St. Louis backfired. The British did evacuate the village, permitting the Americans to build a fort there. The effort to reinforce the garrison was blocked, however, when a sharp defeat was inflicted by the Sacs and Foxes on troops ascending the river in keelboats. Forced out of Prairie du Chien, the Americans suffered another defeat when an expedition commanded by Major Zachary Taylor failed miserably in its mission to destroy the Indian villages that spawned the attacks on the keelboats. When the news of the Treaty of Ghent reached the Mississippi in April, 1815, the Americans were on the defensive and St. Louis was preparing to resist assault.

Emboldened by their successes in 1814, the western Indians were stunned by reports of the treaty, which ignored their victories and placed them on the same footing they had occupied in 1811. In February, 1815, the British had been assuring the Indians that they intended to uphold tribal claims to all land held in 1795 and that great reinforcements had arrived at Quebec to continue the war "on your account." As late as April British agents were ordered to inform the Indians, "That the King their Great Father always true to his promises is resolved not to lay down the [tomahawk] . . . till the Indians are restored to their rights, and their future independence secured."

Within days the British, having official word of peace, were trying to recall war parties they had launched against the Missouri settlements. The British agent's report that the Indians were outraged at the terms of the treaty and in "an extreme degree of excitement" was probably understatement. It took many councils, with British troops standing by alerted for possible trouble, before the warriors were resigned to accepting a peace which negated all their hopes. Desperate to retain some Indian good will and prevent actions which would justify punitive operations by the Americans, the British distributed goods wholesale to their duped allies. Prominent war chiefs were presented coats and pistols, ordinary warriors received ammunition, hoes, and fish spears. But in the end the British had to evacuate Prairie du Chien, Mackinac, and Fort Dearborn, terminating an epoch in Indian history. Never again would the warriors enjoy the armed support of their English Father. But, neither would they again be employed as pawns by the English and Americans in a power game the outcome of which was actually determined far from the frontier and with scant reference to Indian interests. The concept of an Indian barrier state, pushed by the British during the negotiations at Ghent, was quietly interred. From 1815 on, the red man had to deal strictly on American terms.

III

Indian Removal, 1816-1850

Following the War of 1812, the character of Indian-American relations changed. The United States felt less need to conciliate the Indian nations as the threat of British intervention faded, although as late as the 1840's there was official concern over tribesmen visiting Canadian posts. The peremptory demands made on the Indians for more and more land reflected both the weakened positions of the tribes and the flood of settlers to the frontier. Between 1816 and 1848 twelve states entered the Union, scores of treaties were negotiated by which the tribes relinquished the bulk of their holdings east of the Mississippi and consented to removal west, and two Indian wars were fought incidental to the removal policy.

The Indian service which provided the official contact between the two peoples also underwent significant changes. In 1822 the government discontinued its factory system and left the Indian trade to free enterprise after a strenuous campaign by John Jacob Astor and his principal congressional spokesman, Thomas Hart Benton. They argued that the factory system was unfair to private traders and that the government's engagement in economic pursuits weakened its prestige with the Indians. As the Spanish were no longer operating from bases in Florida and Indians were less inclined to visit Canada, reason for the factories had disappeared. Finally, Astor had been able in 1816 to lobby a bill through Congress which restricted licenses in the Indian trade to American citizens, thus ending the privilege which Canadian companies had had of operating below their border.

In 1824 the nucleus of the future Bureau of Indian Affairs was created by the Secretary of War to relieve himself of some tedious detail. The bureau, whose head was officially designated in 1832 as Commissioner of Indian Affairs, originally consisted of a staff of three. These handled the paper work for the three territorial governors acting as superintendents and about a hundred agents, subagents, interpreters, and blacksmiths. As more tribes were brought under United States direction and the normal forces tending toward bureaucratic expansion took effect, the number of personnel increased. By 1850 it was over twice the size it had been in 1824.

March 30, 1834, was an important day for the Indian service; on that date Congress enacted two laws whose impact is still felt. The Indian Trade and Intercourse Act redefined Indian country and strengthened the hand of the government in dealing with intruders. The Indian Reorganization Act was designed to satisfy some of the complaints of "expensive, inefficient, and irresponsible" administration of Indian affairs. Some positions were abolished; the responsibilities of others were altered and clarified. One interesting change was the provision that tribal annuities should be paid to chiefs or other designated representatives instead of individuals within the tribe; the earlier practice had provided a lever for encouraging removal. Paying the chiefs had the effect of emphasizing their position and of strengthening the tribe as an institution, developments subsequent policy-makers abhorred.

The immediate postwar period had found the lately hostile tribes sullen and unco-operative as the agents tried to implement the policies dictated from Washington. Two new army posts were established on the upper Mississippi to keep under surveillance unfriendly Indians in that area, but the growing emphasis on removal kept the tribesmen restless.

Proponents of removal were numerous and vocal. It was apparent that contact with the average frontiersman was not an elevating experience for the Indian. Thus, it could be argued that removal would make possible quarantining the Indian until he could assimilate enough civilization to take his place in white society. Secretary of War John C. Calhoun estimated that thirty years would suffice for the transition, and he and the other official advocates of removal pledged that the new Indian locations would be permanent.

There was virtual unanimity of opinion that agriculture was superior to hunting as a way of life and was a necessary first step for the Indian. As in the 1790's it was accorded divine sanction. A Georgia congressman referred to the "Almighty's command to his creatures to till the earth," and Governor Lewis Cass of Michigan Territory invoked the example of Jacob and Esau. Inspired by the vision of Indians vacating Georgia, Senator Elliot of that state could describe Arkansas as a land "over which Flora has scattered her beauties with a wanton hand; and upon whose bosom innumerable wild animals display their amazing numbers." There were even individuals who invoked the concept of the noble savage and proposed to preserve him from the taint of civilization by moving him beyond it.

Arguments were plentiful that the Indian had to give way as he had no right to block progress—progress being equated with the white man's way of life. Senator Thomas Hart Benton asserted that the whites should supplant the Indians because the former used the land "according to the intentions of the CREATOR." Governor William Henry Harrison, the expert at securing cessions, asked, "Is one of the fairest portions of the globe to remain in a state of nature, the haunt of a few wretched savages, when it seems destined by the Creator to give support to a large population and to be the seat of civilization?" Thus fortified with the knowledge of Divine Will, the officials had no difficulty rationalizing the removal policy.

For the ordinary citizens eyeing Indian land the problem was simpler. The Indians were an encumbrance on the land, "a useless and, perhaps, dangerous population," as one editor described them. The sooner the tribesmen were evicted the better, and there was no hospitality for reformers who talked of civilizing the Indians without removal. One agent's facetious suggestion that a policy of full rations for the tribes would produce disease and kill more Indians than ten times that amount spent on the army was reminiscent of Benjamin Franklin's panacea. The Philadelphian once observed wryly that rum might be the agent of Providence "to extirpate these savages in order to make room for the cultivators of the earth."

Sectionalism also entered the debate over Indian policy. New Englanders who had solved their problem with matchlock and sword a century earlier now deplored the inhuman tactics of Georgians and Midwesterners. Among the missionaries to the Indians, those of New England origin were more inclined to encourage the tribesmen to resist removal. In the debates on removal bills, eastern senators and representatives protested the injustice of the government policies. Massachusetts' Edward Everett attacked Georgia law for leaving the Cherokee "at the mercy of the firebrand and dagger of every unprincipled wretch in the community." Frelinghuysen of New York asked, "Is it one of the prerogatives of the white man, that he may disregard the dictates of moral principles, when an Indian shall be concerned?" From the ranks of the intellectuals Ralph Waldo Emerson protested, "The soul of man, the justice, the mercy that is the heart's heart in all men, from Maine to Georgia, does abhor this business."

As usual, moral indignation over the plight of the red men varied with the distance from him. Those whites avid for Indian land or fearful for their scalps were ever inclined to classify him as subhuman and devoid of rights. Those far removed from the frontier detected great potential in the Indian. A clash between theory and practice occurred in Connecticut in 1824 when a mixed-blood Cherokee youth attending a mission school there married a local white girl from a prominent family. A Connecticut editor expounded on the "affliction, mortification and disgrace" the girl had brought on her family, and the young woman was burned in effigy. The Christian gentlemen who managed the school hastened to ban any further miscegenation.

Probably the most discerning critic of American Indian policy during the period removal was under way was the visitor Alexis de Tocqueville. The Frenchman described how the Americans kindly take the Indians "by the hand and transport them to a grave far from the lands of their fathers." As he observed bitingly, it was all accomplished "with singular felicity; tranquilly, legally, philanthropically, without shedding blood. . . . It is impossible to destroy man with more respect for the laws of humanity." He predicted accurately that the Indian would remain undisturbed in his new home beyond the Mississippi only until the white land-seekers exhausted other possibilities. Then the Indian, exposed to the assaults of "the most grasping nation on the globe," would be driven from one "final" location to another until "their only refuge is the grave."

While the debate went on, the removal policy was being implemented. Numerous treaties negotiated between 1815 and 1830 provided for immediate or ultimate removal. There is ample evidence to indicate that these treaties were of the usual pattern. Bribery was common with chiefs succumbing to a variety of enticements. Lewis Cass in a fit of remorse after one treaty session observed that only orders from the government could induce him to such conduct again. It is little wonder that the Indians became suspicious of any negotiations, for fear they would lead to cessions. Agents found it increasingly difficult to get Indians to place their X's on routine receipts, and there were instances of tribes prescribing the death penalty for chiefs negotiating cessions. But all in vain. The policy which one Commissioner of Indian Affairs referred to as "grand and sacred" was irresistible.

Under Presidents Monroe and Adams the course of events picked up momentum as the Georgia situation approached a crisis. Secretary Calhoun championed removal as a solution to the Indian problem and Monroe approved. Adams was in general agreement but was hampered by scruples. On one occasion he insisted on the renegotiation of a treaty so objectionable to the Creeks that they executed a chief who had co-operated with the whites. President Andrew Jackson was not so sensitive. Reared on the frontier, he embodied its views on Indians. The government's practice of negotiating treaties with tribes as though they were independent nations Jackson early denounced as an "absurdity" and as a "farce." He was completely in sympathy with the removal policy and used his personal influence on some recalcitrant southern tribes. Jackson, arguing that this would relieve the tensions between the federal government and states in Georgia's situation, persuaded Congress to give legislative sanction to the removal policy in the Removal Bill of 1830. This act proposed to bring about the emigration of the Indians at a cost of about $500,000 and provided for an exchange of lands, compensation for improvements, and aid in removal and initial adjustment to their new homes.

Most of the tribes were prevailed upon to remove by the routine methods of persuasion or bribery or threats, or some combination of these. The three exceptions were a band of confederated Sacs and Foxes, the Creeks, and the Seminoles. Back in 1804 the Sacs and Foxes had signed a treaty under suspicious circumstances at the request of Governor Harrison. It provided for a cession of their lands east of the Mississippi, but did not require removal until the line of settlement reached them. Most of the tribesmen were ignorant of their situation until in the late 1820's peremptory demands were made on them to move. Then a faction led by old war chief Black Hawk, who had opposed the Americans in the War of 1812 and had subsequently plagued government agents by his conservative policies, denied the validity of the 1804 treaty.

Ignoring the suggestions of the progressive chief Keokuk,

the malcontents returned to their Rock River village in 1831 only to be evicted by a show of force by regulars and Illinois militia. No blood was shed that year, but in 1832 the return of the band precipitated the fighting dignified in history as the Black Hawk War. For three months the Indians eluded the best efforts of General Henry Atkinson to overtake and defeat them. Meanwhile, they won several skirmishes and terrorized the Illinois frontier. As editors called for a war of extermination, an army which included Abraham Lincoln and Zachary Taylor straggled through the swamps, across the prairies and over the hills. Provoked at the delay in punishing the band, old Indian fighter Andrew Jackson dispatched Winfield Scott to relieve Atkinson of command. Before Scott arrived the Indians were brought to bay as they were about to escape back across the Mississippi, and Black Hawk's band was nearly exterminated. Its misconduct was used to rationalize the extortion of another cession from the Sacs and Foxes.

By the end of 1830 only the Cherokees and the Seminoles among the southern Indians were resisting removal. The Chickasaws, Choctaws, and Creeks had surrendered in the face of action by Georgia, Alabama, and Mississippi which extended state laws over Indians and threatened with fines and punishment anyone blocking removal.

The Cherokees presented a unique situation. Unlike the Sacs and Foxes who staunchly resisted all efforts to civilize them, the Cherokees, led by their mixed-bloods, had made remarkable progress. Grist mills, schools, and well-cultivated fields abounded in the Cherokee country. By the late 1820's a newspaper printed in the Cherokee alphabet was appearing. Although a minority of the tribe was involved, still, they were showing the way for the rest of the Cherokees.

The civilized Indians were dubious that removal would further their interests. As early as 1817 Cherokees were saying that the President confused them. He had been sending them plows and hoes and urging them to abandon hunting. But then the President began lauding the hunting on the Arkansas and offering them rifles if they would emigrate. As Cherokee chiefs later protested to a Senate considering removal legislation, their hope was to be permitted "peacefully . . . [to] enjoy the blessings of civilization and Christianity on the soil of their rightful inheritance."

Evidence of civilization among the Cherokees simply agitated the Georgians. When tribal representatives whom John Quincy Adams described as "well-bred country gentlemen" were in Washington in 1823 on business and Secretary Calhoun appropriately addressed them as "Gentlemen," Georgians were furious. However, even within the tribe civilization had its strenuous opponents. A messiah, incongruously named Whitepath, appeared among the Cherokees to champion a return to the primitive way. The progressive Cherokees united behind blue-eyed, brown-haired John Ross, who was only one-eighth Indian, and squelched this movement. They did it by dominating the National Committee which had been set up earlier to overcome the influence of the towns—the Cherokee equivalent of the state rights movement.

Challenged by a Cherokee constitution establishing a government "having complete jurisdiction over its territory to the exclusion of the authority of every other state," the Georgia legislature acted. Between 1828 and 1831 it brought the Cherokees under state law, abolished their national government except for the purpose of ceding land, declared that no Indian could qualify as a witness in a court case involving whites, and provided penalties for anyone interfering with removal plans. Sealing the doom of the Indians was the discovery of gold in Cherokee country. The gold-seekers who swept over tribal lands were even more contemptuous of Cherokee rights than the usual run of frontiersmen. The agent for the Cherokees brought in federal troops to deal with the intruders, but these were withdrawn when the governor protested to President Jackson that their presence violated Georgia's sovereignty. When the Indians retained former Attorney General William Wirt to represent them, Old Hickory took the frontiersmen's viewpoint that the Indians were just trying to extort a better price from the government and denounced Wirt's actions as "truly wicked."

It became apparent very quickly that the federal courts could not protect the Cherokees. Georgia officials hanged one Indian despite the fact that his death sentence had been voided by a Supreme Court writ. Two New England missionaries to the Cherokees were arrested for refusal to obey a Georgia law and swear allegiance to the state. In 1832 their case was argued before the Supreme Court as *Worcester* vs. *Georgia,* but John Marshall's mandate that federal and not Georgia law ran in the Cherokee country was ignored by Georgia. Jackson's remark, "John Marshall has made his decision, now let him enforce it," may be apocryphal, but it accurately reflects Jackson's refusal to use the executive power to implement the court's defense of the Cherokees. Harassed by the state government, denied protection by the federal government, and urged by its agents to remove, the Cherokees were daily subjected to indignities by the whites. One Cherokee's brick plantation mansion was the scene of a battle. State agents tried to seize it because its Indian owner had employed a white man contrary to state law, but a white squatter already had occupied the ground floor. Caught in the cross fire, the Indian family fled to a floorless log hut in Tennessee. Such tactics finally persuaded a faction of the tribe in 1835 to sign the Treaty of Echota providing for their removal.

In retrospect it is obvious that the Cherokee case was hopeless from the beginning. Their tactic of trying to create a state within a state would have created impossible stresses for the federal system. Had most of the Indians already adopted the ways of the whites, public opinion would not have countenanced the brutal dispossession of the tribesmen. But since the educated Cherokee presiding over a flourishing plantation was the exception, it could be argued that they could not be assimilated in their present condition and for their benefit should be removed to a location where they could be gradually civilized. Indian possession of good land and minerals simply facilitated this type of reasoning.

The Seminole possessions being less desirable, the benefits they could derive from removal were recognized somewhat later. In 1832 the Seminoles were persuaded to sign a treaty which not only called for their removal, but also their union in the West with their relations the Creeks. As the appointed date for removal drew nearer, opposition intensified. Indian orators mobilized the usual arguments against removal and were reinforced by the Negro slaves of the Seminoles. The slaves were unusually influential with their masters and feared transfer to Creek ownership and a more arduous existence. Under the circumstances, the only Seminole band willing to remove was one whose chief stood to profit financially by leading his people west.

Hostilities began in December, 1835, when Seminole extremists murdered their agent and an army officer and ambushed a detachment of troops. For the next seven years the United States strove to crush the sporadic resistance of a few hundred warriors hidden among the swamps and everglades. Hundreds of friendly Indians, thousands of volunteers from neighboring states, and regiments of regulars, failed to root out the hostiles. Not that the whites were hindered by scruple. Zachary Taylor's suggestion that bloodhounds be employed was accepted, and by violating a flag of truce troops finally captured Osceola, one of the principal resistance leaders.

After an expenditure of perhaps 1,500 men and upwards of $50,000,000 the United States ceased formal military operations. Most of the tribe had been removed to Indian Territory, out of which Oklahoma would some day be carved, but several hundred defied the threats and spurned the blandishments and remained in Florida. The only ones who could be said to have profited from this dismal affair were the contractors supplying the troops, and those militiamen whose active duty against the Seminoles might be considered an early form of W.P.A.

It is difficult to generalize on the actual process of removal of the Seminoles and their fellow Indians. The time span covers more than half a century, if the removals from Iowa to Kansas and Kansas to Indian Territory are included. At their best the migrations of the tribesmen resembled closely the pioneering experience of thousands of their white contemporaries. At their worst they approached the horrors created by the Nazi handling of subject peoples.

The tribesmen who moved voluntarily and who were properly equipped and organized, and there were some removals in this category, suffered only the inconveniences to be expected incidental to traveling a thousand miles in pre-Civil

War America. Sometimes, however, these inconveniences were complicated by the ineptness of government agents or collusion between corrupt agents and contractors. Decrepit steamboats were chartered, and salt pork condemned for troop use was issued. The most frightful experiences which led Grant Foreman to employ the term "Trail of Tears" were usually confined to those Indians removed by force. The treatment of some of the Cherokees and Creeks illustrates the appropriateness of the term.

The Creek Treaty of 1832 provided for the cession of that nation's lands east of the Mississippi with the exception of homestead allotments to be made to chiefs and heads of families. These allotments could be sold with the consent of the President. No provision was made for removal but within a short time it was apparent that removal or extinction would be the lot of the Creeks. Not only did the whites disregard all proclamations and orders and inundate the ceded lands, they also secured most of the allotments in an orgy of fraud. An investigator appointed by Andrew Jackson declared, "A greater mass of corruption perhaps, has never been congregated in any part of the world. . . ." But the government was unable or unwilling to defend the red men. When one notorious intruder who had physically abused and looted Indians was killed in a brawl with soldiers, the troop commander decided to cease interfering to avoid trouble with the local whites who had obtained a warrant for the officer's arrest. He excused his inaction on the grounds that he did not have enough ammunition for a general engagement. The officer might have cited the tone of the instructions to the federal marshal in Alabama who was ordered to remove intruders, but to be "concilatory" and do it with due regard to their "feelings and situations." Francis Scott Key got to the heart of the matter with his report to the president that, "the evils of the intruders were caused by the weakness of the United States government in the face of the aggressive actions of the white people of Alabama."

By 1836 the condition of the Creeks was pitiful. Demoralized, they permitted their laws and regulations to be flouted by both races. Crime rates multiplied among the Indians and their society showed every sign of disintegration. At this point a few Creeks chose to retaliate by murdering whites and a "Creek War" was under way. The governor of Alabama labeled all Creeks not in the field against the belligerents as enemies. This was unnecessary, for the friendly Creeks supplied the force to quell the incipient uprising. An Alabama newspaper condemned the war as a "humbug," a "base and diabolical scheme" to justify further crimes against the Indians. The editor summed it up succinctly, "The Red Man must soon leave. They have nothing left on which to subsist. Their property has been taken from them—their stock killed up, their farms pillaged. . . ." But the uprising had served its purpose; the government ordered the removal of the entire tribe.

Even compliance did not free the Creeks from white ruthlessness. When a caravan of 2,000 Indians got under way for the West under the supervision of a marine officer, Alabamians hovered around the column like Cossacks, submitting fraudulent claims and seizing horses and other property from those unable to defend themselves. The government's policy of contracting with private companies to remove the Indians did not improve the situation. The contractors were businessmen out to make a profit, and the rations and transportation furnished the tribesmen reflected this. One decrepit steamboat sank through mishandling, and 311 Creeks drowned. A New Orleans newspaper put the responsibility squarely on the "avaricious disposition" of the contractors who chartered "rotten, old, and unseaworthy boats" and crammed the Indians on "these crazy vessels in such crowds that not the slightest regard seems to have been paid to their safety, comfort, or even decency." The marine was happy that his column suffered only twenty-nine deaths en route to Fort Gibson. But he particularly deplored the contractor's refusal to do anything for the large number who had nothing but a cotton garment to protect them from the sleet storms and no shoes between them and the frozen ground of the last stages of their hegira. About half the Creek nation did not survive the migration and the difficult early years in the West.

Revolting as was the treatment accorded the Creeks, the lot of the Cherokees who were removed forcibly was worse. Thousands of Cherokees had petitioned the Senate not to ratify the removal treaty negotiated in 1835 by one Cherokee faction, but their petitions were ignored. Three years later an estimated 15,000 of the nation, about three-fourths of the total, were stubbornly clinging to their ancestral homes. General Winfield Scott was given the distasteful task of removing them and went about it systematically. Squads of soldiers were dispatched to surround Cherokee farms quietly and at the point of the bayonet, if necessary, bring the residents into stockaded concentration camps. A missionary described graphically, "The poor captive, in a state of distressing agitation, his weeping wife almost frantic with terror, surrounded by a group of crying, terrified children, without a friend to speak a consoling word. . . ." Driven from his home and possessions, he was unable to prepare for the trip facing him or to dispose of his property profitably. Jackal-like local whites accompanied the squads and immediately fell on the abandoned property, looting and burning.

Divided into parties of about a thousand, those Cherokees who had not escaped to become the nucleus of the band in North Carolina today were started westward under armed guard. Conditions varied from one party to another, but sickness, poor rations, bad roads, and inclement weather were common. Statistics on the mortality rate are incomplete, but one estimate is that more than 4,000 Cherokees died in the removal. In the midst of the sufferings of the emigrants President Van Buren reported to Congress that the United States handling of Indian Affairs had been "just and friendly throughout; its efforts for their civilization constant, and directed by the best feelings of humanity; its watchfulness in protecting them from individual frauds unremitting. . . ."

Tragic as was the well-publicized fate of the Cherokees and Creeks, there were other tribes, such as the Winnebagos, who suffered as much or more and their story has never been told in detail. Like other tribes from the Midwest, these Indians suffered the agonies of removal more than once. Between 1829 and 1866 the Winnebagos ceded land in seven different negotiations, involving six possible changes of residence. The original pressure on the tribe, whose principal villages lay south of the Wisconsin River, came from the lead-miners who invaded their lands in the 1820's. The "violent rabble," as one United States official termed them for their disregard of Indian rights, precipitated a minor frontier incident, the Winnebago War. That, following the usual script, led to the Winnebago sale of their rights to the lead-mining area in 1829.

When a few aided Black Hawk in 1832 the tribe was required to sell its remaining fertile acreage south of the Wisconsin River and agree to occupy the Neutral Ground in Iowa or move north of the Wisconsin River. But the Winnebagos procrastinated, few caring to assume the mission of a barrier between those inveterate enemies, the Sacs and Foxes in Iowa and the Sioux to the north. Ironically, the Winnebagos whom the Americans had penalized for aiding the Sacs and Foxes in the Black Hawk War were now in deathly fear of those Indians who resented aid other Winnebagos had provided the whites.

In constant dislocation for the next thirty years, shifted from one place to another, the Winnebagos deteriorated as a tribe and degenerated individually. Their population declined perhaps 50 per cent as disease and dissipation took their toll. "Miserable and degraded," "profligate, worthless and vindictive," and "besotted" are terms recurring in official reports on the tribe. Although the Winnebagos sold all their remaining land east of the Mississippi in 1837 and agreed to remove to the Neutral Ground, it required the presence of troops in 1840 to expedite their change of residence. By 1845 most of the Winnebagos were back in Wisconsin or on a strip of land along the west bank of the Mississippi which they occupied in defiance of the treaty.

For several years the government had tried unsuccessfully to get the tribe to consent to removal to Kansas. By 1841 the objective had changed to getting the Winnebagos to join other tribes in a new Indian territory to the north. Government officials were now attributing Winnebago difficulties to their "enormously large" annuities and "the want of proper guards to protect them against the superior cunning and avarice

An Arapaho camp (from a group of photographs by William S. Soule taken between 1867 and 1874, in the vicinity of Fort Dodge, Kansas, and Fort Supply and Fort Sill, Oklahoma).

Smithsonian Institution

Zuni pueblo (photograph by J. K. Hillers, 1879)

of unprincipled white men." In 1843 a Commissioner of Indian Affairs suggested an interesting solution. Since the Indians had only a "possessory right" in the land, the United States should pay them less for it as their numbers declined. Apparently this was a factor considered in subsequent purchases from the Winnebagos.

In 1846 the tribesmen, under pressure, exchanged their claims to the Neutral Ground for a site selected for them in Minnesota which would make them a buffer between the Sioux and Chippewas. Despite a description of their new home as "an excellent and beautiful section of country," it was completely unsatisfactory to the Indians. They did not cherish the role of buffer in Minnesota any more than in Iowa, and five years after they had presumably located in their new home there were less than two hundred Winnebagos in residence there. Unaccustomed to the rigorous climate, discouraged by the heavy growths of timber and the poor quality of the soil, and intimidated by the Sioux, the Winnebagos drifted back to Iowa and Wisconsin. Recognizing the impossibility of keeping the tribe so far north, the government first located them on the Crow River and, when settlers protested, next located them on the Blue Earth River in Minnesota. The Winnebagos seem to have been relatively satisfied for the first time and their agents reported a marked improvement in their condition. But the cruelest blow yet awaited them. White settlers envied the Indians their fertile acres on Blue Earth River and forced allotment of homesteads and the sale of the surplus acres. In this fashion approximately half the original reservation went to the whites. The policy was offered, of course, as of benefit to the Indians—giving them "greater incentive to personal exertion and industry." However, the government for three years failed to provide agricultural implements promised, presumably on the assumption that the Winnebagos' days in Minnesota were numbered.

They were. The settlers seized upon the Sioux Uprising of 1862 as a pretext for forcing the completely innocent Winnebagos to trade their Minnesota acres for a reservation in South Dakota at Crow Creek. Under pressure from western congressmen and dealing with a Secretary of the Interior who declared it "quite absurd for the government to bargain with them for lands to which they have no title," Congress summarily dispensed with the treaty fiction and ordered the removal of the Winnebagos from Minnesota.

Once again the harried tribe migrated westward to a new home. Despite optimistic reports on their new reservation at Crow Creek, it became evident quickly that the tribe would either have to be subsisted or would starve. The local troop commander reported that the land would produce a satisfactory crop about once in five years, there was no game in the vicinity, and the neighboring Sioux were hostile. As the Indians began to plan escape from this dead end, the government decided to issue them rations—at their expense. Every other day the Indians lined up to be doled out small quantities of a nauseous concoction of flour, water, a few beans, and chopped lean beef, entrails, and heads brewed in a huge open vat. The ration was so vile that the Indians, who were certainly less discriminating in their fare than the whites, could not eat it. In desperation the tribesmen began to slip away, most of them to the Omaha reservation in Nebraska but some to their old Wisconsin haunts. Belatedly recognizing the injustice done the Winnebagos, the government negotiated to permit them to share the Omaha reservation and Congress eventually compensated them for the costs of the last removal. Meanwhile many of the tribe struggled for existence along the Wisconsin River in the midst of a growing white population.

If the years between the influx of miners on their land in the 1820's and the Winnebagos final location in Nebraska in the 1860's were a completely shattering experience for the Indians, the whites had profited. The licensed traders had done well at the expense of the tribe, permitting the unsophisticated Indians to run up large debts and then getting the debts written into treaties. Indeed, if the traders were not taken care of, there would be no treaties, for the traders had great influence with their customers. Compared with the licensed traders who numbered in their ranks some of the leading business and political figures of Wisconsin, Iowa, and Minnesota, the other whites who preyed on the Indians were a shabby assortment. Predominating were the proprietors of the grog shops that infested the border of the Indian country, bootlegging liquor to the Indian for his annuity blankets, flour, and pork. As elsewhere on the frontier, apparently defrauding the unsophisticated red man did not constitute a violation of any ethical or moral code.

Whether Winnebagos, Cherokees, or Chippewas were involved, the panacea offered by government officials for tribal troubles was removal. An examination, however, of the condition of the tribes in their new homes leads one to conclude that they could hardly have been worse off if they had remained subject to the whites in their ancestral homelands. The prairie and plains tribes that had been inveigled into surrendering some of their land to make room for the immigrants resented the newcomers. The introduction to the region of nearly 100,000 Indians, many of whom depended in part upon hunting, definitely upset the fine balance between wild life and Indian population in that part of North America. Those Indians native to the eastern edge of the plains complained that the buffalo had been driven so far west that they "got very hungry before they could overtake them."

As early as 1816 clashes were occurring between the western tribes and the migrating Indians. The Chickasaws who arrived west of the Mississippi in the 1830's were not able to take up the lands originally assigned them for fear of the "wild tribes." The United States sent commissioners, peace councils were held, cavalry was introduced into the army to cope with the new conditions on the plains, but the difficulties persisted as long as there were buffalo to quarrel over. The Comanches not only resented the newcomers but blamed the United States for introducing them. The Osages raided the livestock of the immigrant Indians who were making inroads on the game that had sustained that tribe. The Pawnees, who were a terror to the newcomers, were driven to take action by the Sioux who were pressing them from the north at the same time that the eastern Indians were beginning to crowd in.

Much of the fighting that went on does not substantiate the reputation of the plains tribesmen as the fiercest warriors on the continent. Better armed, the eastern Indians more than held their own. In 1853 in the most highly publicized of the battles about a hundred Sacs and Foxes, who had recently moved to Kansas, stood off a thousand plains Indians out to exterminate buffalo-hunting parties from the east.

Unfortunately, the United States did not live up to its pledges to protect the immigrant Indians in their new locations any better than it had met other responsibilities to them. When weapons promised the Indians were not delivered on schedule, they were helpless to defend themselves against the exasperated Comanches or Osages. Sufficient troops were never available to protect them; in 1834 there were less than three thousand along the entire western frontier. Thus, the Indians whom the United States was theoretically trying to wean from their warlike ways either had to revive these qualities or be overrun. But the cult of the warrior was still strong among the immigrant Indians. Not only did many of them willingly take up the challenge of the plains and prairie tribes, but four hundred Choctaws once agreed to serve as auxiliaries against the Seminoles. When the United States failed to meet the terms they had expected, some of the four hundred joined the Mexicans against the Texans. The Texans also appreciated the fighting ability of the immigrant Indians and tried to recruit aid against the Mexicans.

It is little wonder that the removed tribesmen failed to make the progress predicted so blithely in the halls of Congress and the columns of the newspapers. They frequently had to revert to their old fighting ways to survive. Their political and social unity had been shattered by the factionalism inflamed by treaty negotiations. They were demoralized by the loss of friends and relatives in the holocaust of removal and debilitated by illness, dissipation, and sheer loss of hope.

The program for civilizing the Indians centered upon the Civilization Fund, an annual sum first appropriated by Congress in 1819. Shortly after the War of 1812 private groups had secured permission to work among the southern tribes. Their success led to the creation of a fund of $10,000 to be expended annually on civilizing the Indians. As no administrative machinery existed for the task, the government circularized church and benevolent societies, inviting them to seek subsidies from the fund for schools which they would operate. This approach was quite successful. By the late 1840's the government was still appropriating only the $10,000 annually, but private groups and the tribesmen themselves were pouring over $150,000 into schools which had sprung up in all the tribes that would accept them. In addition, for years treaties carried provisions for the establishment of model farms, the erection and maintenance of grist and saw mills, and the location of white mechanics and blacksmiths among the tribes.

The House committee which recommended the original appropriation in 1819 neatly summed up the philosophy underlying the program: "Put into the hands of their children the primer and the hoe, and they will naturally, in time, take hold of the plough . . . and they will grow up in habits of morality and industry. . . ." The extinction of the tribal system and communal ownership of land would inevitably follow. Within one generation, predicted the first head of the Bureau of Indian Affairs, the tribesmen would be civilized. He was a poor prophet. By 1850 considerable progress was apparent among some Indians, particularly those now called the "Five Civilized Tribes," but even here it was quite uneven and other tribes had apparently made virtually no progress. Several factors help explain this.

First was the resistance of the Indians themselves. The mixed-bloods were the most amenable. The full-bloods generally were more firmly attached to the old gods and the old ways. The memories of the removal experience and contact with the whisky peddlers along the frontier had made many of them skeptical about the virtues of the way of life being pressed upon them. Forced through removal to revert to living by the rifle and the tomahawk, some were so embittered by the experience as to suggest that the missionaries might well devote their talents to improving the morals of their fellow whites before becoming too concerned over the red man's fate.

As game disappeared and their annuities became the only assured source of income, the Indians were happy to share in the produce from the model farms. But it was a rare tribesman who was inspired to brave the taunts and jibes of his fellows and devote himself to agriculture. Besides, the location and operation of the farms and mills frequently seemed designed to profit white men rather than Indians. These jobs constituted political patronage, and rotation in office was an accepted principle.

Nor were the Indians without fault. The factionalism which always plagued the tribes both intensified the opposition to the civilization program and in part sprang from it. Those who had first moved west of the Mississippi opposed the later arrivals, the mixed-bloods were at odds with the full-bloods, and there were treaty and non-treaty factions stemming from the unsavory negotiations authorizing removal.

Competition among the missionaries themselves sometimes hurt the cause. It was confusing and disillusioning for the Indian forced to choose the one gospel from the several presented for his approval. The results reflected the similar situation among the white Protestants. The relatively educated mixed-bloods elected most frequently to be Presbyterians. The more primitive full-bloods were attracted to the Baptists, who frequently employed Negro and Indian pastors. The Methodists drew from both.

American Indians

Most of the missionaries and teachers were selfless, dedicated people who labored uncomplainingly and were relatively unrewarded. Unfortunately, the contempt many of them felt for Indian culture did not prepare them for their work. There were instances of individuals, like the Pawnee agency employees in the 1840's, whose superiority complex was so overwhelming that they did not hesitate to inflict corporal punishment on Indians for minor transgressions of a code alien to the red man. Taking roasting ears from the agency garden did not constitute a crime to the Indians, but it did to the white men. It was reminiscent of the Puritan's efforts to enforce sabbatarianism among New England tribesmen.

For the relatively advanced Five Civilized Tribes the issue of slavery complicated matters. By the late 1840's abolitionist church workers from the North were running into more and more opposition. Expulsion from the tribal area was not unusual, and the governments evolving among the Five Civilized Tribes began to legislate against abolitionists and the practice of teaching slaves to read and write. Although slaveowners were a small minority among the tribes, they generally dominated the new governments. In time this led some missionaries sponsored by northern groups to turn over their responsibilities to their southern brethren who did not find slavery and Christianity incompatible.

The friction resulting from these controversies hindered the program for civilizing which lacked proper administration at best. Those groups receiving assistance from the Civilization Fund were required to submit annual reports, but standards and objectives varied greatly. By the 1840's officials preferred the manual labor school which featured the three R's plus the household arts for the girls and agriculture and mechanical arts for the boys. Nevertheless, there were a few schools which continued to stress academic subjects, including Greek, Latin, and astronomy.

Another area of dispute featured the proponents of the day school versus the advocates of the boarding school. The latter enjoyed official favor as it brought the child under the discipline of the school for the full twenty-four hours. Pupils in the day schools frequently had very poor attendence records once the novelty wore off, and parental interest was lacking. The fact that school schedules allowed for Christian holidays and the harvesting of crops but not the indispensable buffalo hunts did not improve the situation.

These school problems were typical of the difficulties plaguing relations between the Indians and the United States in the period after the War of 1812. Where cultural values conflicted, the superiority of the Bible, the primer, and the plow were never questioned by the whites and no attempt was made to compromise with Indian tradition. However, even the most sanguine of the reformers must have had their misgivings about the virtues of civilization. Those Indians who were making the most "progress" were also displaying a more highly developed acquisitive instinct and were losing the generosity and loyalty which were the finest characteristics of their native culture. Too frequently it appeared that in the transition from one culture to the other the Indian retained the worst features of both.

IV

The Warriors' Last Stand, 1840-1876

While the eastern tribes were being mangled by the removal process, the plains tribes were enjoying a fleeting burst of prosperity. Mobilized by the white man's horse and sometimes armed with his weapons, these tribesmen blossomed into the prototype of the American Indian. Their first American contacts were Lewis and Clark and the fur traders and trappers who followed them. But these mutually profitable contacts were submerged in the first wave of prairie schooners headed for the Far West. By 1841 Oregon had begun to attract emigrant trains, in 1846 Texas entered the Union, and in 1848 the Mexican cessions to the United States by the Treaty of Guadalupe Hidalgo brought scores of new tribes under American jurisdiction.

The wave of wagon trains across the plains in the early 1840's turned into a flood in the 1850's. The Indians watched dismayed while the emigrants and their stock destroyed timber and pastures along the streams and frightened away the buffalo herds. Incidents multiplied as the tribesmen hung around the caravan routes, driving off stock at every chance and killing an occasional white who had ventured too far from his companions. The whites retaliated by indiscriminate killings inspired by revenge and sheer nervousness. The guilty whites and Indians seldom paid the price for their misdeeds; it was simpler to blame an entire people for the excesses of a few.

As the competition for the buffalo stiffened, tribes like the Comanches, Navahos, and Apaches stepped up their raids on the Texas and Mexican settlements. That these people, particularly the Mexicans, were now under the protection of the United States was difficult for the plains tribes to comprehend. The Navahos protested that their trouble with the Mexicans antedated the American difficulties and had not been settled by the Treaty of Guadalupe Hidalgo. The Apaches put it quite bluntly, "We must steal from somebody; and if you will not permit us to rob the Mexicans, we must steal from you or fight you."

One clause in the Treaty of Guadalupe Hidalgo made the United States liable for damages done to Mexicans by Indians living in the United States, but government agents were incapable of breaking raiding habits of long standing, and there were not enough troops to do the job. One realistic agent only asked that the Comanches follow routes into Mexico which would bypass American garrisons.

Relieved of this liability by a clause in the Gadsden Purchase Treaty of 1853, government agents still had their hands full with complaints from Texans, emigrants on the plains, and residents of New Mexico. The Texas problem was particularly thorny because of the benefits Texans anticipated with annexation. One Texas editor in late 1845 predicted confidently that "the giant arms of the United States will soon sweep the few bands of hostile Indians from our borders." However, thirty years were to pass before settlements in northern and western Texas were free of the Comanche threat.

As early as 1845 Major Phil Kearny negotiated with Indians on the Platte in an attempt to free the emigrant trains from attack. In 1849 Forts Laramie and Kearney were established to guard the Platte River route, heavily traveled since gold discoveries in California. Several new routes west had been opened up, and Indians who had been undisturbed by the Oregon and Sante Fe trails now found their buffalo ranges invaded by gold-inflamed whites. In pursuit of new strikes, hardy prospectors spread into every nook and cranny of the West.

Once again the gods seemed to take the white man's side. In the quarter-century before the Civil War several epidemics swept the western Indians, sapping their power to resist. Smallpox ravaged them in four epidemics, 1835–60, and cholera was the menace in 1849. Estimates of casualties are frightful. Of 1,600 Mandans, only about 100 survived a smallpox epidemic which also struck down perhaps half of the Blackfeet. More than half of the Kiowas and Comanches were the victims of Asiatic cholera, and other plains tribes suffered proportionally. It is interesting to speculate on the extent to which this eased the American penetration of the plains. Cholera and smallpox notwithstanding, the Indians would have ultimately been crushed, but the process would have been bloodier and more protracted.

Aside from the attempts to mediate between the emigrant tribes and the plains Indians, the first United States negotiations with the latter came in the early 1850's. At Forts Laramie and

The Warriors' Last Stand, 1840–1876

Atkinson plains tribes defined their territories, pledged to refrain from hostile actions, and were promised annuities. On paper, at least, the problem was solved. But the marks of a few headmen on a scrap of paper could not change a way of life, even if the Indians had comprehended the new political relationship between the United States and Texas, the nature of precise boundaries, and the tender American concern for the settlements in old Mexico. Less understandable is the United States cavalier handling of the Fort Laramie Treaty of 1851. The Senate cut the duration of the annuities and when the Crows refused to ratify the change, the omission was ignored and the treaty promulgated.

For the army the era brought new problems. Infantry could garrison the new posts, but the foot soldiers lacked the mobility to patrol the emigrant routes and run down hostiles. Supply was as important a problem as manpower. It cost about $35 a month to maintain a horse at Fort Laramie on grain from the East, but cavalry were indispensable on the plains. They demonstrated their worth in strikes against the Teton Sioux and Comanches and by 1861 the latter were temporarily on the defensive.

The sedentary Indians of the Southwest, such as the Pueblos, Pimas, and Papagos, also had to adjust to the new conditions produced by American occupation. For them it was not difficult since they managed to retain most of the autonomy they had enjoyed under the Spanish and Mexican governments. Their principal interest in the Americans was to obtain protection against the Navahos and Apaches.

To the north the Indians of the Nevada and Utah deserts were brushed aside by the emigrants and miners who invaded their homeland. Operating at a subsistence level in small bands, unable to offer more than token resistance, they were the prey of both the whites and the plains Indians who raided their camps for slaves.

On the Pacific Coast the tribesmen were little better equipped to resist the flood of Americans. In California the mission Indians presented the most pitiful spectacle. After seventy years under the benevolent despotism of the mission system, in 1833 they had been suddenly thrown on their own resources when the Mexican government secularized the missions. The step was defended as a freeing of the Indians from clerical control but was designed to exploit the wealth of the missions. Just as many of the ex-mission Indians were beginning to adjust to their new situation as servants on the estates of Californians, the Treaty of Guadalupe Hidalgo set the stage for another crushing blow. Many of their Mexican patrons lost their land in the next decade, and the Indians were set adrift once more. About one-tenth of the mission Indians survived this callous treatment at the hands of the Mexicans and Americans.

In the 1850's American agents, seeking to revive something similar to the mission system, got cessions from the California tribes and promised the establishment of reservations. This was the first major experiment by the United States along this line. But, the Senate refused to ratify most of the treaties on the grounds that the United States had purchased California and the natives had no usufructuary rights in the land. Not until 1944 did their descendants receive compensation from the United States, a total of more than $5,000,000 for the wrong done their ancestors.

In Oregon, Washington, and northern California the natives had been in contact with white traders for years, and with the usual results. The iron tools and weapons and the demands of the traders had altered their way of life. For those who escaped the deadly new diseases the change had been beneficial. But beginning in the 1840's settlers began to arrive in the Pacific Northwest and within twenty years the usual wars had been fought, the usual peace terms imposed, and the Indians shunted off to reservations. As one commissioner wrote matter-of-factly, "That these reservations will cause any considerable annoyance to the whites we do not believe. They consist, for the most part, of ground unfitted for cultivation, but suited to the peculiar habits of the Indians." There they could nurse their wrath pending a final outbreak.

Nowhere were the pressures on the American Indian any greater than in Indian Territory, that area west of Arkansas and Missouri which Calhoun and his contemporaries had conceived as the final resting place for the Indians removed from the eastern United States. In Missouri agitation developed as early as 1844 for the opening of a white corridor to the West through the Indian country which had been created by presumably inviolable treaties. The Mexican War and United States territorial acquisitions resulting from it brought new pressures on the Indians by 1850.

As the tribes in Kansas began to receive feelers about new cessions, congressmen began to debate Stephen A. Douglas' proposal for the organization of Nebraska Territory. The politician's capacity for accommodation was fully realized in the debates over the bill to destroy the Indian country which many of these men had helped create a generation earlier as the "final" home for the red men. The usual claims about Divine Will and the inevitable progress of the white man were brought out, and the usual rumblings of conscience troubled those least concerned—with one exception. Unlike the New Englanders, Texas' Sam Houston in protesting this proposed injustice to the Indians was running counter to strong sentiments held by his constituents.

Among the Indians concerned, native tribes like the Pawnees and Kaws and emigrant tribes like the Delawares and Miamis, there was the customary inability to resist the proposals made to them. As usual, government agents presented the plans for new cessions under the guise of tribal interest. They argued, as they had with the Winnebagos in this period, that the tribes held more land than they could use and the surplus was a constant temptation to the whites. The solution was new treaties which would establish diminished reserves and in some instances allot farms to individual Indians. The surplus land would be held in trust by the Office of Indian Affairs until it could be sold and the proceeds credited to the tribal account. In 1854 alone, twelve treaties resulted in the cession of nearly 18,000,000 acres to the United States: the Indians retained less than 1,500,000 acres of their original holdings.

The net result of this program for the Indians was described in 1857 by the Secretary of the Interior as "disastrous." Pro- and anti-slavery forces in Kansas might feud among themselves over the future of Kansas, but they closed ranks to deal with the red men. As one orator remarked in the debate over the Kansas-Nebraska Bill, "While the Senate Chamber rings with stirring appeals upon the subject of the wrongs of the African, the wrongs of the Indian are passed by in silence."

Their access to the diminishing buffalo herds hindered by white land holdings between them and the plains, the Indians were being pushed helter-skelter into an agrarian way of life which they neither understood nor desired. In some instances chiefs were induced to approve the expenditure of tribal funds for shoddily constructed houses which their people then declined to occupy. The empty structures littering the reservations did nothing but enrich the contractors and provide glaring evidence of the stupidity or venality of officials administering Indian policy.

Meanwhile, the Kansans engaged in an orgy of looting and intimidation unequaled since the Georgians harried the Cherokees a generation earlier. Once again the federal government failed to protect the rights and property of the Indians. Missouri's Senator Thomas Hart Benton even issued a map which designated certain Indian lands as open for settlement. The Commissioner of Indian Affairs denounced it as a fraud, but frontiersmen had already been encouraged to infiltrate and local officials were sympathetic. The first territorial governor of Kansas actively speculated in Indian lands. Another, in his inaugural address, advised expelling the Five Civilized Tribes from eastern Oklahoma, arguing with brutal frankness, "The Indian treaties will constitute no obstacle any more than precisely similar treaties did in Kansas. . . ."

The Indians did not welcome the Kansas governor's advice on organizing a territory. A few of the educated mixed-bloods had already been alerted by the annexation of Texas. The Cherokee newspaper predicted emigrants to Texas would want to pass through the Indian country, white settlements would surround it, and then "a Commissioner will be sent down to negotiate, with a pocket full of money and his mouth full of lies. Some chiefs he will bribe, some he will flatter and some he will make drunk; and the result will be . . . something that will be called a treaty. . . ."

In the period between the Mexican and Civil wars several

bills were introduced into Congress to organize a federal territory or territories in the country held by the Five Civilized Tribes. The Indian leadership opposed this, fearful of the consequences for their culture and institutions. They could delay, but they could not halt the juggernaut. As one official estimated the situation, "Necessity will soon *compel* the incorporation of their country into the Union, and before its stern requisitions every other consideration will give way, and even wrong find, as it ever does, in necessity its apology." The author of these sentiments was Elias Rector, who as southern superintendent helped lay the groundwork for the disaster that overcame the Five Civilized Tribes during the Civil War.

That the Confederate States of America should find allies among the Cherokees, Creeks, Seminoles, Chickasaws, and Choctaws in the West was only natural. Their tribal leadership was drawn from the ranks of the mixed-bloods who frequently held slaves and identified themselves with the South. The agents and agency employees were products of a patronage system that allotted these plums to Arkansans and Texans. After the withdrawal of Union garrisons from Indian country south of Kansas the tribesmen had no alternative but to deal with the Confederacy, which surrounded them on three sides. Indeed, the failure of the United States to provide protection for the tribes absolves them of much of the blame for their defection. Finally, Confederate agents made effective use of a statement in the 1860 campaign by Republican William Seward advocating another removal of the Five Civilized Tribes.

Nevertheless, the Indians were no more in agreement on the Civil War than on any other subject. Only among the Choctaws and Chickasaws was there a clear majority favoring the

South. Elsewhere, many of the inarticulate full-bloods voted with their feet by retreating into Kansas or Missouri when their leaders affiliated their tribes with the Confederacy. Among the Cherokees more warriors served the Union, and about as many Creeks remained loyal. The schisms that occurred ordinarily followed the lines previously established by tribal factionalism. The full-bloods who had opposed removal treaties were more frequently secessionists. The principal exceptions were Stand Watie, an almost fullblood Cherokee and a bulwark of strength for the Southern cause, and the nearly white John Ross, who spoke for the full-bloods who accepted secession reluctantly, if at all. It is apparent that most of the Indians left to their own devices would have remained neutral. One band of Kickapoos accomplished this by retreating all the way from Indian territory to Mexico.

The treaties the Indians signed with the Confederacy incorporated some of the changes the Indians sought in their relations with the whites. They secured control of traders within their boundaries and the right to tax them, police power rested exclusively with the Indians, and the Confederate States of America was made financially liable for the actions of intruders. That the change to gray uniforms had not completely metamorphosed human nature is evident in the direct relation between the strength of the tribe and such concessions made to it. And the Creek treaty contained that old persuader, a secret clause providing a bribe for an influential headman.

Neither the South nor the North considered the area west of the Mississippi an important theater of war or made much use of their Indian troops except as scouts and skirmishers. More than four regiments of Indians were organized by Confederate agents, but only at Pea Ridge were they employed in the battle line. Their lack of discipline and training discouraged any further use of the Indians. Their principal accomplishment at Pea Ridge was to inspire charges of brutal and inhuman treatment when they resorted to the tomahawk and took several scalps. The view of the Indian held by the professional soldiers was expressed by the Union officer who advised that the Indians in blue be discharged and put to raising crops.

If their military contributions was slight, the losses they suffered were not, and the Cherokee Stand Watie had the distinction of being the last Confederate general to lay down his arms. Casualties were heaviest among Watie's tribe and were not confined to the battlefield. Conditions in the refugee camps in Missouri and Kansas took a heavy toll as did the guerrilla warfare which ravaged the Indian country after formal military operations ceased there in 1862. Bushwhacking, burning, and looting were the order of the day and the Creeks and Cherokees bore the brunt. Driving off Indian cattle became a profitable business in which Union officers, prominent Kansans, and even Indian Service personnel were implicated. An estimated 300,000 head disappeared in this fashion. More difficult to assess is the damage done by fear, suspicion, and hatred fostered among the tribesmen by the internecine warfare. Previous rifts were deepened, and new ones opened to plague the Indians into the twentieth century.

Long before federal troops were once again in possession of the Indian country west of Arkansas, settlers and speculators in Kansas were looking upon it as the answer to their own Indian problem. As early as 1862 the Kansas delegation to Congress was pressing the administration to shift Kansas' Indian population south. To be sure, the Confederacy then controlled the area and the tribes there had treaties which guaranteed them possession, but these same tribes, or at least factions within them, had conveniently allied themselves with the Confederacy. The Commissioner of Indian Affairs asserted that the tribesmen "had compromised their rights under existing treaties" and afforded the United States a "favorable opportunity." Congress hastened to avail itself of the loophole and in 1863 authorized negotiations with the tribes in Kansas for their removal.

It is probable that many of these Indians, intimidated and persecuted, were ready to resume their travels. But it cannot be maintained that the tribesmen in the Indian country were eager, or even willing, to receive them. The Five Civilized Tribes were given no choice in the matter. Ignoring the fact that federal troops had abandoned the Indian country leaving the tribes there no option but to co-operate with the Confederacy or abandon their homes and property, the United States in 1866 extorted new treaties from the Five Civilized Tribes. These penalized the innocent with the guilty and cost the Indians about half of what is now Oklahoma. The tribes had to agree to the admission of Kansas and plains Indians to their territory and provide tribal memberships for the newly freed slaves. The railroad interests were taken care of by provisions for right of ways through the Indian nations. Paradoxically, the Creeks and Cherokees, who were rather evenly divided in their allegiance in the late war, were saddled with more onerous treaties than the Chickasaws and Choctaws, who were overwhelmingly Southern in their sympathies. To climax the injustice of the proceedings, the Secretary of the Interior, who subsequently left office after being investigated for malpractices, sought advice from the very ex-Confederate agent who had led the tribesmen astray! He had not been penalized for his role in the Civil War, but the ex-Confederate approved the harsh terms meted out to the Five Civilized Tribes. As was demonstrated earlier in Kansas, the whites could ally against the Indians when they could get together on nothing else.

In petitioning for removal of the tribes from their state, Kansans had emphasized the benefits the Indians would derive from removal. Concentrated, for example, they would be easier to Christianize and protect. Seldom in official statements were the more sordid reasons advanced. However, in 1867 a Topeka newspaper reflected grass roots sentiment, in describing Indians as "a set of miserable, dirty, lousy, blanketed, thieving, lying, sneaking, murdering, graceless, faithless, gut-eating skunks . . . whose immediate and final extermination all men, except Indian agents and traders, should pray for."

Included among the reasons for ridding Kansas of its tribal population was a fear that they might be inspired by the Sioux uprising in 1862 to unite for one last stand against the whites. The Sioux outbreak falls into the usual pattern. Generations of the eastern or Santee Sioux had known the whites only in the guise of missionaries, traders, or government officials. Not until the 1840's did the tide of white settlement begin to lap at their boundaries. In the next twenty years the eastern Sioux surrendered most of their land in Minnesota and retired to reservations. But, like the Winnebagos, they did retain some of the best land in the state. This and the friction engendered by Indians and whites in close contact produced the customary crop of incidents. The climax came in 1862, when one band, inspired by the oratory of the malevolent Little Crow and irked by the delay in the payment of annuities they had come to depend upon, took to the warpath. Joined by other warriors, they soon had a force of over a thousand and murdered and raped, burned and looted their way through the Minnesota Valley. Like Pontiac, Little Crow could inspire but not control, and the Indian attacks had no unity. The tribesmen were captured or routed, but not before they had killed about five hundred settlers and soldiers and detained in Minnesota half the troops that state raised during the Civil War.

Punishment was quick, harsh, and indiscriminate. Thirty-eight Santee Sioux were featured in a hanging bee at Fort Snelling. Payment of annuities to all Santee Sioux was stopped for the period 1863–66 and they were removed from the state, although many had remained quietly at home and some had actively supported the military operations against their own people. Tribal funds were drawn upon to pay claims for damages despite the report of an investigating commission that whites were guilty of much of the looting of the abandoned farm homes and that losses were generally exaggerated. Wits observed that enough rutabagas were reported lost to cover the state a foot deep.

An incidental result of the uprising in Minnesota was to aggravate an already potentially dangerous situation as Santee Sioux laden with loot and escorting white prisoners took refuge among the plains tribes. In the far Southwest the Navahos and Apaches had taken the withdrawal of Federal garrisons after the firing on Fort Sumter as a signal to harry the settlements and wipe out small parties of prospectors and travelers. The Confederate governor of Arizona advocated killing all Apache warriors and enslaving the women and children. Jefferson Davis repudiated the policy, but a Federal official made the extermination of the warriors one of his objectives and he was not rebuked from Washington.

The legendary frontiersman Kit Carson was commissioned

a colonel to lead the expeditions against the Apaches and Navahos. Intimidated by his relentless pursuit the Mescalero Apaches agreed to locate on a reservation. The Navahos, after suffering several hundred casualties and seeing their crops destroyed and sheep butchered, did the same. For the Navahos this was the end of a way of life. Never again, although frequently under severe provocation, did they pit their strength against the United States.

Confederate agents were only a minor factor in the unrest on the southern plains. Having received no annuities for two years because of bureaucratic bungling, the Kiowas were ready to sign a treaty with the South, as were some of the Comanches. The Confederates had no ambitious plans for offensive operations involving the plains tribes; their intention here as elsewhere was simply to keep the Indians passively allied to them. The South, however, would profit by any dissension between the United States and the Indians.

The rush of settlers into Colorado following the strike near Pike's Peak had provided the southern plains Indians ample grievances, and the Civil War offered them an opportunity for reprisals. Not that the plains tribes needed an excuse for going to war. The introduction of horses and iron weapons had given them the time and means to indulge their belligerent proclivities. Status seekers among these tribes sought opportunities to steal horses, count coups, and collect scalps. Slipping into the midst of an enemy encampment and stealing a horse, or striking a foe's body with a coup stick at the risk of one's own life carried more prestige than the routine slaughter of a score of the enemy. War was more a game than a technique for exterminating another people. This explains both the plains Indian's militance and the emphasis on individual action which negated most of his operations. Lacking was the discipline which could enforce sentry duty, carry out adequate reconnaisance, or prevent one eager young warrior from uncovering an ambush by a premature charge. Nevertheless, the soldiers found the plains Indian a formidable foe, daring in attack and elusive in retreat. Even when burdened with camp equipage and family he was rarely overtaken. Retreating Indian bands had a habit of melting away as the troopers overtook them, scattering to reunite after the heavy cavalry mounts were exhausted, and the troopers had to return to the plodding pace of their baggage trains.

Summer, after the buffalo herds had been stalked to replenish the tribal meat supply, was the Indians' favorite time for warfare. By June, 1864, the combination of provocative actions by the white intruders and repeated and unwarranted attacks on Indian camps by Federal troops had stimulated among the Cheyennes and Arapahoes an unusual burst of activity. Although technically restricted to a reservation on the upper Arkansas River, they had followed the buffalo herds that summer and, incidentally, raided isolated ranches and stagecoach stations. They murdered one family within twenty miles of Denver. The victims' bloated and festering corpses, hacked and scalped, were drawn through Denver in the bed of a wagon. They served to dispel any lingering doubt about the only good Indian being a dead Indian. Colorado's governor called out the militia, but the red men easily eluded pursuit.

Tiring of the game and ready to settle down for the winter, one band led by Black Kettle and Little Antelope reported to Fort Lyon on the upper Arkansas. Having made their peace, they retired to Sand Creek about forty miles away. Here late in November, 1864, a column of Colorado militia commanded by Colonel J. M. Chivington, a Methodist minister, caught them unawares and perpetrated the notorious Sand Creek Massacre. Disregarding the previous negotiations at Fort Lyon which the Indians had presumed restored them to American favor, the frontiersmen showed no mercy. Of the band of five hundred, perhaps a third, mostly women, children, and the aged, were killed by the surprise charge through the camp. The militia rivaled the Indians in their brutality. Eyewitnesses told of children clubbed and pregnant women disemboweled. Their stories inspired torrents of protest in the East and would have resulted in Chivington's court-martial had he not meanwhile left the service. General Nelson A. Miles termed the massacre the "foulest and most unjustifiable crime in the annals of America." In Denver, where he exhibited a collection of a hundred scalps between acts in a local theater, Chivington was a hero and public benefactor.

Recountings of Sand Creek around campfires led to a fresh wave of Indian attacks, but the tribesmen burned themselves out by the fall of 1865. Treaties negotiated with the southern Cheyennes and Arapahoes and the Comanches and Kiowas located the tribes on even smaller reservations and brought temporary peace to the southern plains.

Teton Sioux, reinforced by the northern Cheyennes and Arapahoes, presented an even greater threat in the 1860's. They had the same provocations and the same opportunities. The white encroachment which the Teton Sioux under Red Cloud reacted to most violently was the opening of the Bozeman Trail during the Civil War years. In an effort to improve communications with Montana mining camps, the army was directed to safeguard a new route which ran through some of the favorite Sioux hunting grounds, territory guaranteed the

Indians by treaty. Forts were erected, but the garrisons left them at the risk of their lives, and precious little freight and few emigrants traveled over the Bozeman Trail. Red Cloud's infuriated warriors spread their attacks to other emigrant trails and joined the southern plains tribes in the raids which brought mail deliveries and stagecoach operations virtually to a halt in the summer of 1864. Massive punitive expeditions in 1864 and 1865 accomplished little except to delight the contractors. One column required fifteen steamboats to supply it and the head of the Interior Department estimated that it cost $2,000,000 a year simply to maintain a regiment on the plains.

Since its creation in 1849 the Interior Department had been charged with the conduct of Indian affairs. When the Indians went on the warpath, however—and at any given moment from 1850 to 1880 this was the case somewhere on the frontier —the army was brought back into the picture. Army personnel accused the Interior Department officials of coddling the Indians and arming them with weapons superior to those carried by the troops. Army partisans in Congress and the press denounced the "mawkish sentimentality" of the humanitarians and derided the bronchial clergymen who sought expense-paid opportunities to inspect the West. Stung by eastern charges of harshness and brutality, frontiersmen victorious in a skirmish decorated Indian skulls with inscriptions such as "I am on the reservation at Last" and "Let Harpers Tell of My Virtues."

But even in the West there was disagreement. Some felt the army was protecting the railroads at the expense of the immigrant trails and the isolated settlers. William Tecumseh Sherman, who commanded in the West following the Civil War, retorted that millions were being spent to protect a handful of settlers who should give up their exposed locations. He also suggested that some sections of the country were living off the military posts established there to protect them. It was true that some frontier politicians still regarded an Indian war as a God-sent opportunity to don their militia uniforms and channel a little federal money into their region.

When in the Fetterman Massacre the Sioux ambushed and cut to pieces a small detachment of troops on the Bozeman Trail, public opinion, temporarily aroused, demanded a re-assessment of Indian policy. During the next decade there were investigations and some policy innovations, but not the revolutions needed to bring substantial improvement.

In 1867 a Peace Commission of distinguished civilians and officers toured the plains and submitted a report which placed most of the blame on the whites. This ultimately led to the abandonment of the Bozeman Trail, one of the rare retreats the Indians were able to inflict on the advancing whites. The commission's other recommendations included the usual solutions relating to reservations and private property. Their suggestion that the treaty process for negotiating agreements with tribes be abandoned was adopted in 1871 because it coincided with the insistence of representatives that the House have an equal voice in Indian affairs with the Senate.

Shortly after he took office, President Grant tried to improve the quality of the agents by employing army officers and the nominees of religious denominations. Congress quickly terminated the experiment with the officers, but the other continued through Grant's administration, to taper off after he left the White House. In theory the idea of drawing the agents from lists of church nominees seemed very attractive. In practice it did not work nearly so well as expected, although some improvement was noted. Known as the "Quaker Policy" for the denomination to which Grant first turned, it suffered from the difficulty of recruiting able and honest people to serve for a niggardly compensation in remote spots among an alien people. Leaders of the Dutch Reformed Church were reduced to canvassing the student body of Rutgers to find someone to take over the San Carlos Apache! Protestants had never enjoyed much success in their missionary work among the tribesmen and found harvesting souls in Africa and the Orient more rewarding. The Catholics, who had been supplying more than half the funds expended, felt themselves discriminated against. They were asked to nominate agents for only a few of the reservations where they had formerly operated and were to be banned from the others even for missionary work. This fostered dissension among the religious leaders which helped bring to an end an experiment which the reformers, among them the personnel of the new Board of Indian Commissioners, had enthusiastically indorsed.

The Board of Indian Commissioners was established by Congress in response to a general demand for a non-partisan organization to oversee the administration of Indian affairs. Staffed by distinguished reformers who served without compensation, the board had authority only to audit, inspect, and recommend. Early in its sixty-five-year history the board was frequently at odds with the Interior Department, but as the board personnel resigned themselves to seeing much of their advice go unheeded, relations improved. That board members themselves were not infallible was proved when one of them became Commissioner of Indian Affairs. He was subsequently ousted for offering favors to an Indian agent to aid the commissioner's son in securing a silver mine. Another Commissioner of Indian Affairs to resign after a House committee rebuked him for incompetence was the only Indian who had held the post, Ely S. Parker, a Seneca and a former staff officer with Grant.

Had the reformers been completely virtuous and also omnipotent, they would have been unable to eliminate the conflicts on the plains in view of the remorseless advance of the whites. The best the Board of Indian Commissioners could recommend was honest administration of Indian funds and supplies, which was certainly lacking, further detribalization, and the introduction of agriculture and concepts of private property. Even if implemented, the policies would not have prevented clashes between aggressive whites and the harried tribesmen who clung to their old hunting grounds.

After the creation of the Peace Commission in 1867, there was time for one generation of Indian wars before the passing of the buffalo and the advent of the railroad and rapid-fire weapons combined to end that great American institution. In the plains south of the railroad corridor the Red River War was the last major campaign, but to the southwest the Apaches were militant into the 1880's. In the Great Basin the Utes went on the warpath in 1879 and farther west there was the Modoc War in 1872–73 and the Nez Percé outbreak in 1877. On the northern plains the Sioux troubles culminated in the major operations of 1876–77.

The Red River War of 1874–75 was fought seven years after the Peace Commission presumably had located the southern plains tribes on reservations. Regardless of treaties signed, a majority of the Indians had not been ready to give up their free way of life in 1867. Nor was the government prepared to receive them; even the Quaker policy could not always produce agents that were both honest and able. Confronted with a shortage of rations on the reservations, unwilling or incapable of raising crops to supplement the issue, the bands continued to hunt buffalo and, when they became scarce, to raid settlers' herds. Some wild bands refused to come into the reservation at all and stepped up their attacks on the outlying Texas settlements. Thousands of head of cattle were stolen to be traded to the Comancheros, the New Mexican traders who supplied the wild bands with arms and ammunition and trade goods. The warriors also found it profitable to capture whites and hold them for ransom.

In dealing with the problem, the army found it very difficult to distinguish between hostiles and friendlies since any village might contain both. The soldiers were also caught between the anguished cries of the settlers and the insistence of the Interior Department officials on the peace policy. But warriors like the Kiowas Satank and Satanta remained impervious to moral suasion, and even some of the Quaker administrators sympathized with the Texan who thundered, "Give us Phil Sheridan, and send Phil-anthropy to the devil."

The tactics which broke the back of the Indian resistance were winter campaigns and relentless pursuit. George Custer had demonstrated at the Battle of the Washita that troops could operate in the dead of winter when the Indians were accustomed to consider themselves immune from attack. Phil Sheridan incorporated winter operations in his campaign which sent converging columns against the Kiowa, Comanche, Arapahoe, and Cheyenne bands that declined to prove their friendliness by returning to the reservation. In a dozen engagements the troops scattered the Indians across the frozen plains. By spring of 1875 the last hostiles were ready to come to terms.

As they reported in, their pony herds and weapons were confiscated and a number of warriors were held for trial. Seventy of them ultimately were sentenced to detention in Florida.

Unlike Satank and Satanta, who chose death to submission, Quanah Parker elected to adjust. The son of a white captive and a Comanche war chief, he had participated in the attack on the hated buffalo hunters at the Battle of Adobe Walls. Now, with what was remarkable vision for an Indian, and he was thoroughly Indian in culture, he recognized that the disappearance of the buffalo and the vigor with which army operations were being pushed made the old ways impossible. With his collaboration the wildest of the Comanche bands came in to the reservation, and peace came to the southern plains.

The Apaches also felt the weight of the new policy. By 1875 reservations had been established for them, but only the western tribes appeared ready to settle down. Among the eastern Apaches the Chiricahuas furnished most of the hostiles, although their leaders attracted support from other Apache tribes. Victoria, Nana, and Geronimo led the braves that terrorized the Southwest for fifteen years. Seldom in bands of more than a hundred, traveling lightly and living off the land, they struck viciously in one area and reappeared twenty-four hours later a hundred miles away. Masters of ambush, they kept pursuers wary. Five thousand troops were in the field when Geronimo finally surrendered his little band of thirty-six to end the Apache wars.

West of the Rockies the Utes, Modocs, and Nez Percés provided the most excitement in the last round of Indian wars. The belligerency of all three originated primarily in Indian resentment at being restricted to smaller and less desirable reservations—even those not free of white intruders. A humorless, dedicated reformer turned Indian agent helped precipitate the Ute outbreak and concluded his career with a stave driven down his throat and his wife the temporary concubine of Ute warriors. A contributing factor to the Modoc uprising was an attempt to arrest chieftain Captain Jack for murdering a medicine man.

The Modoc War was the most protracted of the three, for the hostiles took refuge near the California-Oregon boundary in lava beds which offered excellent defensive positions. In terrain resembling something in outer space the Modocs held out for six months, meanwhile violating a flag of truce to murder two peace commissioners and leave Agent Alfred B. Meacham for dead. Four of the Indians involved were ultimately court-martialed and hanged. Captain Jack resisted all efforts to convert him before his execution. In vain he offered forty ponies to a divine, who had been assuring him of the existence of Heaven, to replace him on the scaffold which offered a short-cut to this eternal bliss.

No Utes were hanged following their uprising, but their Washington-appointed chief, Ouray, had to approve cession of all their holdings in Colorado. Things had worked out much as the governor of Colorado had proposed: a brief Indian war had been fought, and at minimum cost the Utes had been expelled from the state.

In contrast with the brutality and treachery, by white standards, which characterized Ute and Modoc operations, the Nez Percés fought a most un-Indian war. There was no scalping, and mistreatment of civilians was at a minimum. One leader, Chief Joseph, had succeeded his father as the head of the conservative faction among the Nez Percés. Old Joseph had been a Christian for many years, only to destroy his New Testament after some typical treaty shenanigans by the whites. His son was uncompromisingly pagan and his followers may have been influenced by Smohollah, a Paiute messiah who promised the resurrection of all dead Indians and game animals and the total destruction of the whites. Young Joseph did not seek war, but when some of his unruly followers precipitated it, he fought a masterful campaign featuring a thousand-mile retreat in the face of superior forces. His conquerors were lavish in their praise of his generalship, and he was probably the only defeated Indian chief ever to be feted at a banquet shortly after his capture. Contrary to their expectations, however, the defeated Nez Percés were forced to take up temporary residence in Oklahoma, where unaccustomed climate and slipshod treatment took a heavy toll of the band.

To the east of the Nez Percés the hostile Sioux, northern Cheyennes, and northern Arapahoes stunned the Americans with their success in the summer of 1876 against the army's *beau sabreur*, George Armstrong Custer. Following their success in forcing the Americans out of the Powder River country in 1868, the northern Indians had been subjected to unremitting pressure to settle down on reservations. The Blackfeet, after cavalry had massacred a friendly band by mistake on the Marias, ceased to resist. Most of the Sioux located at one of the four big reservations in the Dakotas and Montana, but there were some wild bands, led by chiefs like Sitting Bull, Gall, and Crazy Horse who refused to trade their freedom for the dubious security of the agency. They picked up recruits of similar mind from northern Cheyennes and northern Arapahoes and were joined every summer by Indians happy to trade the enervating monotony and short rations of the reservation for the free life of the buffalo hunters.

The ancient formula produced trouble on the northern plains as it had elsewhere. White men were lured to the area by rumors of mineral wealth, despite treaties binding the United States to keep its citizens off the Indian land. In defense of prospectors who banded together to invade the area in 1870, a Wyoming newspaper pontificated, "The same inscrutable Arbiter that decreed the downfall of Rome, has pronounced the doom of extinction upon the red men of America. To attempt to defer this result by mawkish sentimentalism . . . is unworthy of the age."

Giving way before the demands of the gold-seekers, the government dispatched troops under Custer into the Black Hills in 1874, purportedly to locate sites for army posts, although the column was accompanied by prospectors. Custer reported the area a gold-seeker's paradise and the pressure mounted.

The Indians did not interfere with Custer in 1874. It was rarely possible for them to overcome the divisive influences inherent in their loose political organization and present a united front to the invaders. The remarkable thing is that they were able to combine against Custer two years later.

The intervening summer had seen the miners filtering into the Black Hills, being taken into custody by the army, and then being turned over to civil authorities to be freed. The usual situation had developed; the government was incapable of protecting Indian rights against its own citizens. The time-honored solution, short of war, was to purchase the area in dispute, but the Indians set too high a price. Consciously or otherwise, the government took the next step by authorizing the army to operate against bands which ignored an ultimatum to come into the reservation. The United States could not maintain discipline among its own people; nevertheless, it was always ready to employ its army to harass and punish wayward red men.

Unfortunately for the Seventh Cavalry one basic error was committed: the strength of the hostiles was drastically underestimated. Sitting Bull and Crazy Horse were reported to have only about 150 lodges with them. But, the village which spewed warriors to annihilate Custer's column contained several hundred more lodges of Indians who had joined Sitting Bull and the hostiles after wintering at the agency. These tribesmen succeeded where the southern Cheyennes had failed at the Battle of the Washita. Custer had gained a victory there by maintaining the initiative. Out of character was his failure to push the charge against the Indians at Little Big Horn, which gave time to rally and overwhelm him.

The Indians reacted to their success with their habitual vacillation. Instead of maintaining the initiative, they squandered their well-earned victory celebrating and hunting. When the temporarily stunned army resumed its offensive the Indian forces broke down into bands and melted away. Some skirmishing occurred, but by the next spring all of the hostiles, except those who followed Sitting Bull and Gall into Canada, trailed into the agencies to be dismounted and disarmed. Like their brothers on the southern plains they had reached the limit of their power to resist. William Tecumseh Sherman attributed the change in the situation on the plains to the construction of the railroad net which could carry troops in a day as far as they could march in a month. Others emphasized the disappearance of the buffalo herds before the guns of the professional hunters. Quite early, General Sheridan had discerned their contribution to the solution of the Indian problem and events bore him out. The southern herd dissolved into miles of putrescent carcasses in the 1870's, and by 1885 buffalo herds were gone from the northern plains. Among the Indians, chiefs like Red Cloud had learned the unlimited strength of the whites by visiting the East; others like Crazy Horse had had to learn the hard way. Cheyenne and Sioux blood would be shed again, but not under the illusion that the march of the white man could be halted.

The end of the Indian wars marked the conclusion of a long chapter of American history. For nearly three centuries the threat of the scalping knife and the tomahawk had haunted the settlers on the frontier. Wars and rumors of wars had contributed much to the determination of western personality and political and social organization. What unity there was on the frontier, together with the tendency to look to federal authority, was due in large part to the Indian problem. It had also furthered political careers. Generations of Indian fighters had capitalized on their reputations at the polls, as was exemplified by Andrew Jackson and William Henry Harrison. And in their way Indian wars had been an economic boon to the frontier. One estimate in 1870 was that each Indian killed in these wars had required an expenditure of more than $1,000,000.

Among the tribesmen the youths no longer could aspire to emulate the Satanks and the Galls, whose successes against the whites and hostile tribes had made them top men in their tribal hierarchies. No longer could an elderly warrior like the great Shoshoni Chief Washakie confound his critics and rejuvenate his prestige by disappearing to return days later with scalps taken in single-handed exploits against the enemy. No longer would the village turn out to welcome home their trophy-laden warriors and dance for days to honor their heroes. The entire status structure among those Indians had been uprooted.

V

Acculturation under Duress

Between 1850 and 1934 proposals for civilizing the American Indian were many. Most of them were old standbys—Christianize the aborigines, educate them, and introduce them to private property. The variable factor was the condition under which these policies would be applied. The 1850's saw the concept of an Indian country shattered by the rapidly growing white population and the railroad net devised to serve it. Then large reservations came under attack and the land base of the tribes was further whittled down. Until the 1880's proposals to concentrate the Indians in Indian Territory and a comparable area in the North had strong supporters. During this period at least twenty-five tribes were located in what is now Oklahoma, and many others were shifted to new locations. Quite apt was the barbed question of the great Sioux chief Spotted Tail, "Why does not the Great Father put his red children on wheels, so he can move them as he will?" With businessmen happy to part with as much as $20,000 to secure the contract to ration tribes during removal one reason for the popularity of the policy is obvious. Only the well-publicized misery of the Cheyenne, Ponca, and Nez Percé removals to Indian Territory terminated this unfortunate practice.

The plight of the removed Nez Percé has already been mentioned. The Poncas, a small tribe transferred against its will with the usual rise in the tribal death rate, had a vociferous champion in journalist and former minister T. H. Tibbles. Touring the country with the Indian girl Bright Eyes, he advertised the plight of the Poncas and also won the maiden's hand in marriage. There was no such romance in the Cheyenne case. Those tribesmen from the northern plains were located in Indian Territory only to be decimated by malarial fevers. A shortage of medicine and food complicated their situation. Of the meat rationed to them their agent could only say, "it was not grossly bad." Concluding that to remain in the South meant a slow death, the Cheyennes under Dull Knife and Little Wolf elected to defy the whites and make their way back home. Thousands of troops were summoned to cope with a small band of about three hundred Cheyennes, only about one in five of whom was a warrior. In the face of steadily mounting odds the party fought its way north, leaving a pitiful trail of dead, wounded, and debilitated Indians. The band under Dull Knife was captured, only to break out once more in a final death spasm. Little Wolf's party wintered in Wyoming and then surrendered and was permitted to remain in the North.

Tales of the suffering of Cheyennes, Nez Percés, and Poncas fell on more and more sympathetic ears in this period. Parts of the West which had been clamoring for blood in 1865 had passed through the frontier stage by 1880 and had developed a humanitarian interest in the red man. But the rule enunciated by Senator Plumb of Kansas that sympathy with the Indian increases proportional to the distance from him still seemed to apply. Typical of the attitude of most Westerners was an Iowan's comment on the local reservation Indians, "They are as worthless as so many tamed wolves." The center of agitation in behalf of the Indian continued to be the East.

Before the Civil War interest in justice for the Indian had run a poor second to concern for the welfare of the Negro slave. The postwar period was one of general lassitude and apathy on the part of the reformers. The general public was certainly in no mood to launch new crusades. Former Agent Meacham campaigned for Indian reform by displaying gunshot and knife wounds inflicted by the treacherous Modocs in 1873, only to be regarded as a crackpot by Americans intent upon their pursuit of the almighty dollar.

Prodded by the frightful reports of Indian and white battle losses and the deadly attrition of Indian population incidental to the shuttling of the tribes from location to location, the American conscience slowly awakened. Recitation of the wrongs inflicted on the Poncas recruited the vitriolic pen of Helen Hunt Jackson. Critics have damned her lack of balance, even suppression of facts that did not fit her preconceptions, but in *A Century of Dishonor* and *Ramona* she publicized the Indian cause as it had never been publicized before.

Around 1880 the growing interest in Indian welfare produced several organizations. One, the National Indian Association, was promoted primarily by women. From its headquarters in Philadelphia it sponsored missions among the tribesmen and its state chapters bombarded Washington with petitions. Another, the Indian Citizenship Committee of Boston, was a by-product of the Ponca fiasco and labored to secure political rights for the red men. Most influential was the Indian Rights Association organized in Philadelphia by two young men, Herbert Welsh and Henry S. Pancoast. From the beginning it earned respectful attention by its on-the-spot investigations which it publicized in thousands of pamphlets. Officials who ignored them were made aware of the association's objectives by a lobbyist maintained in Washington.

In a class by itself was the National Indian Defense Association founded by Dr. T. A. Bland, publisher of the *Council Fire*. Bland and his associates opposed policies which would rush acculturation. Alone among the reformers they looked askance at the attempts to detribalize the red men and emasculate the chiefs. Red Cloud, the leader among the non-progressive Oglala Sioux, inspired and was inspired by Bland.

An unofficial co-ordinating agency for the reformers was the Lake Mohonk Conference instituted by the Quaker educator Albert K. Smiley, a member of the Board of Indian Commissioners. From 1883 until his death in 1912 he sponsored annually a conference at his resort which attracted government officials, congressmen, and reformers. Out of their sessions came programs which subsequently inspired much criticism, but which then represented majority thinking of friends of the Indian. The policies they recommended were those which guided administration of Indian affairs during the next quarter-century.

Regardless of the excellence of policies devised, in the final analysis their efficacy depended upon their administrators. And Indian Service personnel too seldom were both honest and able. Grant's Quaker policy and his brief experiment with army officers recruited many honest and well-intentioned agents, but too frequently they were totally ignorant of the culture of the people they were supposed to administer. The folly of selecting agents from among people who had never seen an Indian seems not to have been understood. A much more essential qualification in the eyes of those who made the appointments was the political lineage of the appointee. One successful applicant for the Blackfeet agency proved so worthless that a party leader pronounced the ultimate in condemnations, "His character is such that he ought not to hold office even if a Republican." The Democrats were less guilty only in that they were seldom in a position to make appointments. Such criteria provided instructors in agriculture who had never farmed, clerks who couldn't write, and teachers too dissolute or incompetent to hold positions in other schools. But it is perhaps unrealistic to expect better appointments at the lower levels when the average term for Commissioners of Indian Affairs seldom exceeded two years.

One might well wonder at the attraction the agency positions seemed to hold. Top pay in the 1880's was about $1,500 a year for service in some remote spot under obvious disadvantages with every expectation of brief tenure. Yet there was never a shortage of applicants. The answer can perhaps be found in the commonly held belief that a few years as an Indian agent would guarantee the fortune of anyone not overly burdened with scruples. In an era of United States history when the acquisitive instinct reached perhaps its highest development, as seen in the careers of the Daniel Drews, John D. Rockefellers, William Marcy Tweeds, and Roscoe Conklings, the Indian Service opened vistas of opportunity. The

devices employed to defraud the Indian, or to manipulate services to him to further financial interests of certain parties,
ranged from crude theft to refined questions of ethics.

Did the location of agencies with an eye to profiting certain
communities rather than benefiting the Indians constitute corruption? Obviously many businessmen, bulwarks of respecta-
bility in their communities, did not think so. When the issue
of transferring an agency from Camp Apache to San Carlos
arose, it was damned as a conspiracy to replace New Mexican
contractors with Arizonans and Californians. The issue was
discussed as though the principal consideration was the profit
to be made from supplying the reservation.

There was no room for doubt about the ethics of some of
the practices on reservations. At San Carlos the agent had been
devoting his time and effort to mining operations which he
partially supported by food and materials diverted from the
agency warehouses. The agent not only escaped prosecution
but sold a mine to the inspector sent to check on him. The
inspector in turn involved the son of the Commissioner of
Indian Affairs in his mining venture.

Another agent sent to guide the Apaches along the white
man's road stocked his ranch with government cattle and sold
to local fences the blankets and other supplies designated for
the needy Apaches. He also permitted considerable latitude to
his subordinates. The agency blacksmith and carpenter spent
much of their time on private projects, the former even charging for shoeing the mounts of government scouts.

Contracting to supply an Indian reservation was a lucra-
tive business. Collusion between contractor and agent provided
"steel chopping knives made of cast iron; best brogans with
paper soles; blankets made of shoddy and glue, which fell to

pieces when wet . . . forty dozen elastics . . . when there was not a stocking in the tribe." Collusion between ranchers and lumbermen on the one hand and agents on the other resulted in herds fattening on Indian grass and contracts being filled with Indian timber. Honest mistakes were as damaging. Sawmills were erected miles from any timber; bakeries were built which the Indians declined to patronize; agency farms were opened where drought was a chronic condition.

In the light of such blundering or outright fraud by white Christians, the Indian resistance to the feeble missionary activities is understandable. Although the expenditures of church groups increased over what they had been in the early nineteenth century, the record was still quite spotty. A Chinaman on the banks of the Yangtze remained a more romantic and challenging figure than the sullen, syphilitic aborigine squatting in the dust of his allotment. When the reservations were parceled out for missionary activity, some of the tribes were completely neglected by the denominations to which they had been assigned. Former Commissioner of Indian Affairs George W. Manypenny protested that Americans were expending millions of dollars on foreign missions while the total budget for Indian work did not exceed $10,000 a year.

In contrast to those tribes which attracted no missionaries, there were tribes which had too many. At one time the Sioux at the Rosebud Agency were the subjects of a tug of war between Roman Catholics and Episcopalians which resulted in the ouster of a priest by the agency police. Frequently the sect to be indulged depended upon the affiliation of the agent and this was particularly true during the Quaker policy era.

For the Indian the whole business was most bewildering. He was unable to understand why a change in agency administration might also result in the substitution of an Episcopalian for a Roman Catholic, or a Baptist for a Presbyterian. Moreover, the doctrinal disagreements in which they seemed to delight were as confusing as ever to the Indian. Chief Joseph refused to countenance missionary work among his band, charging, "They will teach us to quarrel about God as the Catholics and Protestants do on the reservation. . . . We may quarrel with men sometimes about things on this earth, but we never quarrel about God. We do not want to learn that."

Roman Catholics seem to have been the most successful in their proselytizing, in part because of the graphic way they presented their message. The Protestant Episcopal Church also enjoyed some success. Their bishops Clarkson, Hare, and Whipple did yeoman work among the tribesmen. Bishop Whipple during the last four decades of the nineteenth century was a one-man propaganda machine, quick to dash off a letter to a wayward congressman or seek an interview with an un-cooperative Commissioner of Indian Affairs. More dynamic than his colleagues, Whipple, or Straight Tongue, as the Indians called him, antagonized many but got results where his less aggressive colleagues would have failed.

Whether Baptist, Roman Catholic, or Presbyterian, the missionaries suffered certain common handicaps. Some of the Christian concepts, such as penance and baptism, were totally alien to tribal religions. There was also a general tendency for the missionaries to extend their operations beyond the spiritual needs of the Indian. They did not feel their mission accomplished until the warrior had not only accepted Christianity, but had given up hunting and raiding, shed his blanket, and settled down to farm an allotment. One denomination demonstrated this by explaining its lack of success at an agency in terms of such mundane matters as frosts, droughts, and cater-pillars.

Some of the missionaries' failures could be attributed to faulty technique and poorly chosen personnel. As one Quaker remarked, "To reach the full-blooded Indian send after him a full-blooded Christian." And even this rare creature would be more effective if he knew the people he was trying to save. Some missionaries worked among a tribe for years without troubling to acquaint themselves with the native religion they were trying to supplant. Religious bigots made little headway with proud tribesmen unimpressed by the quality of the Christianity they were exposed to on the frontier. As one Indian responded to Bishop Whipple's injunction against drunkenness and adultery, "My father, it is your people, who you say have the Great Spirit's book, who bring us the fire-water. It is your white men who corrupt our daughters. Go teach them to do right, and then come to us and I will believe you."

Where Christianity made its greatest inroads, it depended upon the services of native pastors who blended the old teachings with the new, as primitive Christianity had once absorbed pagan practices. Among the Creeks hymns were translated into the native tongue, the social instincts of the people found expression in camp meetings lasting days, and old tribal superstitions showed up in Christian garb. Sermons employing Indian legends to make a point were much more meaningful than those dependent upon parables based on an alien culture.

The more important Indian religious movements which appeared in the late nineteenth century were the peyote cult and the Ghost Dance religion. The peyote cult centered upon the consumption of a non–habit-forming narcotic found in the roots and buttons of a type of cactus. The mild, colorful hallucinations induced by the peyote provided the setting for hymn-singing and testimonials. Most peyote groups grafted this onto Christianity; others emphasized native beliefs. In both forms it spread rapidly from the Southwest, worrying agency officials and missionaries but providing its participants with an outlet for their spiritual urges and a new peace of mind.

In contrast, the Ghost Dance movement was a completely disillusioning experience for the Indians involved. This time it was the turn of the plains tribesmen to produce a messiah movement from the depths of their despair. Like the Delawares of the 1760's and Senecas of the early 1800's, the buffalo Indians were crushed by adversity. As the animals upon which their whole way of life had been based disappeared, as they were alternately threatened and cajoled to exchange the excitement of buffalo hunts and horse-stealing expeditions for the drudgery of the plow and the hoe, the warriors grasped at straws. When their religious leaders reported revelations in which the Great Spirit was critical of men plowing instead of hunting, the Indians eagerly believed them. They echoed the message of Smohollah, the messiah of the Dreamers who had denounced plowing: "Shall I take a knife and tear my mother's bosom?" and mining: "Shall I dig under her skin for her bones?" and haying: "But dare I cut off my mother's hair?"

The plains tribes had produced prophets like Isatai, Pautapety, and Poinkia who promised the return of the buffalo and the annihilation of the whites, but it was a lowly Paiute in Nevada whose message spread like a prairie fire among the buffalo Indians. Wovoka, or Jack Wilson, was a medicine man of no particular pretensions until he fell seriously ill in 1888. On recovery he reported that while unconscious he had consulted the Great Spirit and received a message for his people.

Smithsonian Institution

Geronimo (*far right*), his son, and two warriors (photograph by C. S. Fly, 1886).

Cherokee cabin home in North Carolina (photograph by James Mooney, taken between 1888 and 1893).

Smithsonian Institution

Winnebago warriors (photograph by Upton, 1863)

Similar to the teachings of an older Paiute who may have been his father, Wovoka's communication from on high predicted the plains would again support millions of buffalo and the whites and all their ways would disappear. The Paiute did not claim divinity; he was content to play the role of prophet. Nor did he incite the Indians to drive the whites from the land. He deplored resort to force and instead prescribed dances and songs which would hasten the great day.

By the summer of 1890 word of Wovoka had filtered on to the Great Plains and roused thousands from a slough of despond. The rumor among the southern tribes was that a new Christ had appeared, one dispatched to the Indians—not the whites, who had killed theirs. The Arapahoes were particularly intrigued and sent two of their policemen to verify the story. They returned without having personally seen the messiah but convinced of his existence. In some of the camps all work stopped, and the Indians gave themselves over completely to the Ghost Dance, as the whites termed the ceremony prescribed by Wovoka. The military was alerted to expect trouble on the southern plains, but close surveillance failed to reveal any cause for armed intervention and the excitement gradually subsided.

In the North the fever was higher as the Indians seized upon this ray of hope, and the Ghost Dance attracted thousands of converts in a matter of weeks. The agency officials in some instances allowed themselves to be stampeded. Wovoka's chief apostle among the Sioux was Kicking Bear, who together with other wise men of the Sioux had journeyed a long way to see the messiah. The agent at Standing Rock dispatched police to arrest Kicking Bear for stirring up old Sitting Bull's band. The police returned without the medicine man and too dazed and confused to explain their failure. The power of the new medicine was also attested to by many of the converts who recovered from unconsciousness brought on by fasting and dancing to describe visits with long-dead Sioux who spoke of returning to earth. Warriors also began to prepare shirts bearing magic symbols which would turn aside the white man's bullet. Such developments increased the uneasiness of white settlers and some of the military and Indian Service personnel. When soldiers began to concentrate in the vicinity of the centers of the new religion, some of the enthusiasm for it began to wane. The division among the Sioux which appeared on this issue corresponded generally with the conservative-progressive split.

At the Standing Rock Agency, Sitting Bull's band, which had returned from Canada in 1881, provided a flurry of excitement. The agent had been at odds with the old Sioux leader for years and the Ghost Dance movement only aggravated the situation. Using as a pretext reports that Sitting Bull was preparing to leave the reservation, the agent sent a detachment of Indian police to arrest the old man. Although the Indian police were employed on this mission in the hope that they would arouse less antagonism than troops, the ill feeling between the conservatives and the upholders of the white man's authority may only have worsened a bad situation. The attempt to take Sitting Bull into custody precipitated a burst of violence which resulted in the death of a number of the police and conservatives, including the old Sioux himself.

The death of Sitting Bull did not lead to a general uprising, proof that the Indians, including those who had participated in the Ghost Dance movement, recognized that the day had passed when resistance was practical. The only other serious incident clearly confirmed this.

One band of Ghost Dancers left their agency during the excitement, despite orders to the contrary. To prevent them from joining forces with dissidents at the Pine Ridge Agency, troops were sent to intercept them. When overtaken by Custer's old regiment, the Seventh Cavalry, the Indians were ordered to turn in all weapons. A medicine man fomented opposition among a few diehards which brought the entire band under fire. The result was the Massacre at Wounded Knee. White-manned Hotchkiss guns hurled shells into the milling mob of Indians, and the troops fired their rifles as indiscriminately. Perhaps 250 of 350 Indians were killed or wounded, more than half of the casualties being women and children. Twenty-five troops lost their lives in this, the dying gasp of the plains warriors.

Before it faded away, the messiah movement produced one ludicrous incident. In the midst of the uproar at the Sioux agencies a deranged white man appeared with a message for the Indians. Posing as a messiah, he predicted the millennium would arrive when the star pansies bloomed on the prairies in the spring of 1891. In Red Cloud's Oglala Sioux camp he almost produced a riot before the old chief himself denounced him as a fraud and he was removed from the reservation under armed guard. When the star pansies did bloom the following spring the disillusionment was already complete. Those who had thrilled briefly at the hope of a return to the good old days were awaiting the next move of the whites with resigned dejection.

Ironically, one of the bulwarks of the acculturation policy—

schools—had facilitated the spread of the Ghost Dance. English learned in mission or government schools was the means of communication used to overcome the tribal language barriers. Indeed, the whites first learned of the magnitude of the movement from a mixed-blood postmaster who had been asked to read letters addressed to illiterates. It was a curious product for a policy upon which all reformers agreed.

Despite the general acceptance of the principle, little progress had been made since the first schools were instituted before the Civil War. The average agency school was an unknown quantity, many of them uninspected for years. The teacher frequently was the wife or other relative of the agent and if he or she was competent, it was a coincidence. Even able instructors found it difficult to maintain any enthusiasm in the face of Indian apathy. The only students with good attendance records would be the few mixed-blood sons and daughters of local white men. The full-bloods would attend until something more important such as a hunting trip or a visit to relatives, or sheer boredom, interfered. The reports of the teachers abound in instances of semesters begun with rooms full of eager youths only to have the attendance drop sharply once the novelty wore off.

Until 1870 federal aid for the schools was limited to half-hearted attempts to fulfil treaty stipulations and sporadic efforts to satisfy the reformers. Most of the funds appropriated for the acculturation of the Indians went into pattern farms, mills, and salaries for sundry agency employees. In 1870 Congress appropriated the first sum specifically for the purpose of education. By 1899 over $2,500,000 was being expended annually on 148 boarding schools and 225 day schools with almost 20,000 children in attendance.

Acculturation under Duress

The off-reservation boarding school was most popular in the last quarter of the nineteenth century. Reformers and Indian Service personnel generally agreed that a complete break with the home environment was desirable. Schools like Carlisle in Pennsylvania were the temporary homes of thousands of young Indians. There the youths were encouraged to shed their tribal culture as a relic of the past. With the best of intentions the school administrators did a poor job. Forced to increase enrolment to secure enough federal subsidy to operate, the crowded institutions trained the girls in the operation of laundries and the mass production of food. The boys became skilled at handling farm machinery and adjusting furnaces. None of these tasks had any application to the type of life they would lead when they returned home. If the student did not adapt to the school routine, he was miserable; if he adapted, then he was miserable when he returned to his family. By 1900 every reservation had its quota of returned students who at the same time felt superior to their fellow tribesmen and yet resented being regarded as outsiders by their fellows. One young Sioux, Plenty of Horses, returned from boarding school and sought to regain caste during the Ghost Dance excitement by cold-bloodedly murdering an army officer.

It was another army officer, Captain Richard H. Pratt, who in 1879 had established Carlisle, the best known of the boarding schools. In charge of Indian prisoners in Florida, he was impressed by their adaptability and helped secure admission for some of them to Hampton Institute, a private school for Negroes. At Carlisle, which was supported entirely by federal funds, Pratt introduced the outing system. Coming at the end of the Indian youth's stay at Carlisle, this involved placing the mature student for a period of as much as three years with one of the rural families near Carlisle. Pratt was a strong advocate of assimilation and a bitter critic of contract schools maintained by church groups with government subsidy. The captain maintained that the churches always wanted to return the educated student to the reservation to do church work, whereas Pratt's greatest ambition was to see reservations abolished and Indians completely integrated into white society.

In the 1890's the popularity of the day schools increased. Congressmen preferred them because they were cheaper than the boarding schools, particularly those that were located off the reservation, like Carlisle. It was also argued that the day school did not separate the child from his family and served as a little nucleus of civilization within the tribe. Westerners appreciated it for a different reason but one familiar to anyone who has seen a community mixing God and Mammon in its efforts to attract eleemosynary institutions for the money they bring to the area.

While the boarding school was reaching its peak of popularity, some changes had been introduced into the Indian schools which improved their over-all performance. Uniform textbooks and methods, together with a merit system for teachers, ended some of the grosser inequities among the day schools. The strictly tribal boarding and day schools were brought into the federal system. Some people applauded the government's decision, because of the separation of church and state issue, to cease subsidizing church schools. Others were pleased by the plans to move the Indian children into the public school system as rapidly as possible. None of these changes, however, could convert the apathy of the Indians into a thirst for the white man's knowledge.

Recruiting students for any type of school was always a

problem. Too frequently those children who were enrolled at the distant boarding schools were orphans or from families too low in the tribal hierarchy to resist pressure. Indian parents were understandably reluctant to lose their children for months —or permanently: the death rate among the students was abnormally high. Stories of corporal punishment, of school jails, of young warriors shorn of their long locks heightened the unpopularity of the institutions. To fill the rosters a practice for many years was to deny rations to unco-operative parents or, infrequently, even to imprison them. If this tactic seems harsh, it would be well to note that a contemporary Commissioner of Indian Affairs could defend the requirement on the use of English in the schools by citing as precedent German practices in Alsace and Lorraine. Little wonder that agency police were used virtually to kidnap children for the schools and to guard against truancy. On one reservation the rounding-up of students for the agency school provoked such an outbreak that cavalry had to be summoned to quell it.

The Indian police and the Courts of Indian Offenses were attempts to employ law not only for the purpose of maintaining order and protecting property, but also as an active agent in the acculturation process. When, in 1878, Congress first appropriated funds for agency police, there was ample precedent for their action. The Light Horse, a tribal police force, had appeared among the Creeks before their removal. Among the plains Indians the Soldier societies combined police and military functions, particularly during buffalo hunts. Several agents, John P. Clum being the best example, had evolved their own answer to the law and order problems by recruiting private police forces.

Within six years police forces had been established at forty-eight of sixty agencies. Some officials were critical of the policy and made little use of the police. Many agents, however, came to depend on them for a variety of services. Indian police not only served as truant officers; they also ran down rustlers and bootleggers, acted as messengers, cleaned out irrigation ditches, and took the census. The quality of the personnel varied greatly from reservation to reservation, but as the Quapaw agent summed it up, "They are not perfect, but we could not get along without them at all."

The police were active agents of the acculturation process also. They provided the agent a counter to the influence of conservative chiefs, as Sitting Bull learned at the cost of his life. Policemen were expected to set an example by wearing white man's attire when out of uniform, cutting their hair, practicing monogamy, and taking an allotment after their tribe was introduced to severalty—individual as opposed to communal ownership of land.

For obvious reasons the conservative factions disliked the police. Their duties included such onerous tasks as determining whether a fellow tribesman was working hard enough to merit his sugar, coffee, and tobacco rations. "The police are looked upon as a common foe, and the multitude are bitterly opposed to them," reported one agent. Being saddled in 1883 with the additional duty of judges on the newly established Courts of Indian Offenses did not ease their situation.

The Courts of Indian Offenses were the answer to complaints about the persistence of heathenish dances, polygamy, and the influence of medicine men. Originally police were to serve as judges without additional compensation, playing the roles of both prosecutor and arbiter. On a few reservations they even shared in the fines they levied, an equally dubious practice. Eventually Congress appropriated money to pay the judges salaries not exceeding $8.00 a month, grossly inadequate even by reservation standards.

Like the policemen, the judges were supposed to exhibit the proper progressive characteristics. Unfortunately, the headmen who could command respect as judges frequently were conservatives. And even the progressives occasionally had flaws. Quanah Parker, the former Comanche war chief who became a collaborator after surrendering in 1875, was eventually relieved of his judicial position for a serious lapse. Quanah had too many wives—"five undisputed facts" as his agent referred to them in 1890.

Judge Quanah and his colleagues relieved the agent of many of his burdens as community peacemaker, although the agent reserved the right to review their decisions. From the white man's viewpoint the courts were an asset in eliminating vestiges of the old ways. Whether or not the individual Indian approved depended upon the value he set upon the practices of his ancestors. Even progressives found it difficult to accept the principle that crimes against persons were crimes against society as well and could not be compromised by a gift to an individual. At the other extreme were Indians who adapted so well to the white man's ways that they were soon trying to control the court to advance their interests.

Both policemen and judges declined in number and importance as allotment destroyed the closed reservation and regular law enforcement agencies took over. The elimination of the reservation, this "City of Destruction" as Captain Pratt termed it, was just one of the results of the severalty policy which had been advocated for so long. As noted in chapter ii, American officials had early discerned the advantages of private property in land for Indians. Provisions for severalty were written into a number of treaties following 1850. As with Christianity and education, severalty had almost unanimous support. Scholars were cited to prove that private property had always been the basis of civilization. Local officials urged it to undercut the power of the chiefs. One Commissioner of Indian Affairs, apparently impressed by the activities of the anarchists and labor agitators, emphasized the conservative influence of private property as a counterweight to the "heresies in the social and political world." The familiar argument was employed by a governor of Dakota Territory that a "reasonable quantity of land held . . . by direct grant would not become such an object of complaint or greed as enormous tracts occupied by tribes and claimed by no definite individual." A corollary to this, and a powerful argument for severalty, was the assumption that it would lead to the breakup of the reservations and the sale to whites of the surplus acres after Indians had received their allotments. The Indians' new neighbors were envisioned as examples for the backward tribesman.

Severalty was that rare policy on which Helen Hunt Jackson and the most rabid Indian-haters on the frontier could agree, although for different reasons. Some of its advocates waxed absolutely lyrical. A Sioux agent in 1886 was inspired to visualize the Indian on his allotment, singing as he worked:

> We'll have a little farm, a horse, a pig, and cow,
> And she will mind the dairy and I will guide the plow.

Critics of the policy were few. One senator suggested that perhaps the true principle was not private property but rather that the individual should "own just so much of his mother earth as he can make useful to himself." Smacking of Henry

George's philosophy, this view had little support. Captain Pratt's reasons for supporting severalty were similarly unpopular, but the captain must be given credit for his honesty. He urged it on the assumption that the Indians would soon squander their holdings and then be forced to go to work. There was evidence available that previous experiences with severalty had resulted in something quite like this. Of 1,735 Chippewas granted allotments about 1871, five-sixths of them had sold their lands or been defrauded of them by unscrupulous whites by 1878.

Despite this, the Dawes Severalty Act of 1887 enshrined as general policy what had been taking place piecemeal for years. The law provided that at his discretion the President could allot reservation land to the Indians, the title to be held in trust by the United States for twenty-five years. Full citizenship for the Indian would accompany the allotment. Heads of families were to receive 160 acres with smaller amounts going to other Indians. The surplus, after the Indians had been taken care of, was to go on the market. As written in 1887, the act did not apply to the Five Civilized Tribes and several smaller Indian nations.

The tribesmen did not join in the general rejoicing over the passage of the act. Even among the whites there were a few lingering doubts. Henry L. Dawes, the Massachusetts senator for whom the bill was named, was not enthusiastic. A few months before the passage of the bill he defended it lamely as an attempt to salvage something for the Indians who might otherwise lose all their land to the voracious whites. Grover Cleveland signed the bill, but only after remarking that he agreed with Dawes that the "hunger and thirst of the white man for the Indian's land is almost equal to his hunger and thirst after righteousness." The President promised to be careful to appoint officials who would protect the interests of the Indians in carrying out the severalty policy.

The only concerted Indian opposition to the Dawes Act was expressed by delegates at a convention of representatives from nineteen of the tribes in Indian Territory. The average Indian had not resisted the severalty movement because he either did not understand it or lacked organizations to voice his protest. Not only was the concept of private property in land alien to him, he couldn't even visualize what 160 acres of land was. On one reservation the Indians asked that such a plot be staked out so that they might get some idea of what was involved. When ordered to select allotments, most of the tribesmen dutifully did so, but with no real comprehension of what was involved. Here and there a conservative band would refuse to do even this and their selections were made for them by agency officials. Such a band might negate the principle behind severalty by selecting their allotments in a block and trying to continue the communal way of life.

The Five Civilized Tribes put up the most effective resistance to severalty. They had leaders who could talk the white man's terms, and they were relatively well organized. They were alert to congressional developments and lobbied in Washington. One Cherokee delegation denied to Congress that their tribe practiced communism. "The only difference between your land system and ours," the Cherokees insisted, "is that the unoccupied [land] . . . is not a chattel to be sold and speculated in by men who do not use it. . . . As it is, so long as one acre of our domain is unoccupied," the delegation continued, "any Cherokee who wishes to cultivate it can do so, and make a home, which is his." They predicted that if

Acculturation under Duress

severalty were forced upon them that a few would monopolize the land.

In contrast, advocates of severalty painted sordid pictures of a few sophisticated Indians engrossing the best land under the tribal system. But there was occasional testimony by whites to the contrary. In 1886 the Senate Committee on Indian Affairs reported, "The entire absence of pauperism amongst these tribes and the general thrift of the people are most powerful arguments in favor of their system of landholding. . . ." But the momentum of the severalty movement was too great. In 1893 a senatorial commission came to Indian Territory, and after carefully choosing its witnesses, submitted a report which laid the groundwork for the introduction of severalty among the Five Civilized Tribes.

That the severalty policy was a terrible mistake was apparent shortly after its general application. Some reformers who had pushed it assumed that their job was done and turned to other interests, much as the abolitionists had abandoned the Negro after the Civil War. Despite Cleveland's pessimism about the ability of Indians to succeed at agriculture when experienced white farmers were retreating to the cities, neither he nor his successors reversed the policy. Reservation after reservation was surveyed and allotted, even some where insufficient rainfall made agriculture risky. One is reminded of the Kiowa Chief Little Mountain's sarcastic suggestion that if the President wished corn raised by the Indians he should send them land fit for corn production. Where the land was sufficiently undesirable to whites, as in the desert country of the Southwest, the Indians were not pressured into severalty and there was little change in their pattern of existence.

Prior to its passage, the Creek Chief Pleasant Porter had

doubted that Americans were sufficiently virtuous not to use the Dawes Act to their own advantage. Twenty years later Oklahoma editors were justifying the pillaging of the Indians by such statements as "Sympathy and sentiment never stand in the way of the onward march of empire" and "If they don't learn the value of property and how to adjust themselves to surroundings, they will be 'grafted' out of it—that is one of the unchangeable laws of God and the constitution of man." "Grafted" out of it they were, by tactics that ranged from deceit and duplicity to murder. Had it not resembled what had been happening for three centuries whenever Indian property aroused white cupidity, one would have concluded that some tragic deterioration of American character had taken place.

The first loophole the whites exploited was the act permitting the Indians to lease their allotments. Ignorant of the worth of their holdings and delighted to have any small income which would free them from labor, the Indians leased their land at ridiculously low figures. When members of the Five Civilized Tribes finally received their allotments, real estate agents assisted them in selecting their land and then leased it. The real estate agent made his profit by subletting the property, at a much higher rate, to a white farmer. Most sought after were leases on timber land which could be stripped and, coached by whites, the tribesmen sought many such allotments. What could not be done by conforming to the letter of the law, whites tried to do by circumventing it. On one reservation a gang of illegal leasers defied the police to evict them.

Leasing had been defended as exposing the Indians to beneficial contacts with industrious white farmers. Guardianship, another technique for looting, was offered as a device to protect the interests of minor or incompetent Indians who had received allotments. An enterprising white man with the proper connections would secure appointment as guardian of an incompetent adult, or an orphan, or obtain waivers from a child's parents. Thus in control of the Indian's property he would manipulate it to his own advantage. Outright embezzlement and forgery were not as popular as excessive fees and exorbitant purchases which profited the guardian and his business associates. One white man tried unsuccessfully to secure guardianship of a group of 161 children whose allotments he had planned to select so as to cover a valuable tract of timber.

One particularly underhanded tactic was to inveigle the gullible Indian into writing a will which would assign most of his property to his white friend. This practice perhaps explains a suspicious increase in the number of Indian deaths from undetermined causes. In a few cases murder was definitely proved, the most reprehensible being the bombing of two sleeping children. Kidnapping was yet another weapon in the unprincipled speculator's arsenal. It was sometimes used to facilitate the marriage of a minor, thus qualifying the newly wed boy or girl to sign over his allotment immediately. The wife or husband supplied by the speculator would then disappear.

Several attempts were made to protect the Indian by amending the Dawes Act. The Burke Act of 1906, for example, withheld citizenship until the trust period expired and gave the Secretary of Interior more latitude in handling competency and heirship problems. But as rapidly as the Indian Service personnel closed one loophole, the grafters would discover another. And the apparently limitless possibilities corrupted government officials as well. Judges furthered their careers by selecting the proper guardians; agency officials accepted bribes to expedite allotments which white men hoped to exploit; even the members of the Dawes Commission and executives in the Interior Department were stockholders in companies which dealt in Indian lands. Severalty may not have civilized the Indian, but it definitely corrupted most of the white men who had any contact with it.

Honest administrators, and there were some, found the heirship problem a maze of frustrations. As allottees died intestate, their tracts were assigned to their several heirs, with each death complicating the situation. By 1920 there were allotments shared by over fifty heirs, by 1950 by over a hundred. And any use of the property required the consent of each heir. Countless man hours were expended just trying to apportion the income from leases on such property. Certainly the Indian who was the recipient of several checks, some for only a few cents, was not profiting greatly from the situation. One way out of the imbroglio was to sell the land, but even this could be done only if all of the heirs consented.

Ironically, one of the first persons to impress the allottee with his new status was the tax collector. In some areas the Indians were assessed at excessive rates for all personal property as well as improvements on their farms. The net effect was actually to drive some of them from the community. Far from being a stimulus to civilization, severalty to these Indians seemed to penalize progress. Ignorant of good farming methods, without the credit to purchase the tools and livestock necessary to do the job effectively, and harassed by tax collectors, the average allottee was a failure as a farmer. He had difficulty realizing why he should join the school children in

Acculturation under Duress

celebrating the anniversary of the signing of the Dawes Act.

A small minority, usually mixed-bloods who had already demonstrated the acquisitive instinct, did well by severalty. And there were the "oil Indians" who attracted so much publicity during the twenties, when their allotments sprouted drilling rigs and they were easy targets for the salesmen and swindlers. But for every Indian whose allotment proved to contain oil, there were a score who were reduced to charity cases. Most pitiful were those conservative Indians who as members of tribes had at least enjoyed pride of ownership, and actual use if they desired it, of hundreds of square miles of rolling prairie and wooded hills. Now restricted to an unsought allotment, they usually lost this as soon as alienation became possible. Between 1887 and 1934 the Indians were separated from an estimated 86,000,000 of a total of 138,000,000 acres. Most of that remaining was desert or semidesert: worthless to the white population. Bishop Hare had remarked at the time of the passage of the Dawes Act, "Time will show whether the world or the Church will be more on the alert to take advantage of the occasion." By 1920 the verdict was in. Worldly interests had demonstrated what can happen in a democratic society to property of minority groups incapable of political action.

Administrators were loath to recognize the failure of severalty and the other techniques for civilizing they were trying to apply. As former Commissioner of Indian Affairs Francis E. Leupp summed it up in 1919, "The Indian problem has now reached a stage where its solution is almost wholly a matter of administration." What Leupp and the others found difficult to believe was that the Indian could possibly be better off as a member of a tribal society than as a member of white society. They also failed to take into account cultural diversity among the tribes. Even in the interest of uniform administration it is hard to defend blanket orders to reservation officials to slash food and clothing rations so as to force the Indians to support themselves. The Indians simply did what they had always done—shared what they had and then went hungry together. Equally indefensible was the order from Washington that all male Indians should cut their hair. Some tribesmen believed that their long hair had supernatural significance for rain ceremonies, or that they were doomed if their clipped hair fell into the hands of their enemies. Agents, for their part, regarded long hair as the symbol of resistance to the civilizing program. An agent to the Shoshones referred to it as the Gordian knot. On at least one reservation refractory Indians were shackled so that the hair-cutting order might be carried out.

The only occupations of the white man which the Indian seemed to find appealing were soldier and circus performer. For years tribes like the Pawnee had furnished scouts for the troop columns combing the plains for hostiles. Late in the nineteenth century this practice was regularized, and several all-Indian units were recruited. Although they were not subject to the draft, a number of young men volunteered for service in World War I and acquitted themselves well. As a reward for their services, Congress made all veterans citizens in 1919 (extended to all Indians in 1924), but some of them failed to gain admission to tribal warrior societies. Their elders dismissed the fighting in France as just a shooting war, one in which the individual had no opportunity to demonstrate his manhood by counting coups as befitted a real warrior.

Long after the fighting had ended on the plains, Sitting Bull and many of his contemporaries enacted the role of warriors for the wild west shows. They ambushed stage coaches in stirring finales all over the United States and in a number of European countries. The Indians adjusted quite well to the close-knit circus life and enjoyed the traveling and the part they played. There was some well-founded skepticism, however, about the extent to which this experience helped prepare them for careers in agriculture. Worldly-wise circus hands lounging around reservations were as disruptive in their influence as the old warriors, both classes ready to jeer any Indian who took up woman's work in the fields. Nor did the frequency with which circus Indians were left stranded penniless in remote places endear the practice to the Indian Service personnel who had to figure out a way to get them home.

Soldiering and acting were not encouraged as alternatives to farming, but the Indians in some areas were persuaded to take up stock-raising. But even in this role for which the Indians seemed to be peculiarly fitted, they met with only indifferent success. At one extreme were the tribesmen who looked upon their herds of cattle or flocks of sheep as they had once regarded their pony herds—as status symbols. As their holdings multiplied, overgrazing resulted. At the other extreme were the Sioux who were persuaded to sell their cattle during the World War I boom, only to squander their capital and lapse into poverty.

Friends of the Indian who were willing to face the facts must have been at their wit's end by 1925. Policies undertaken in the nineteenth century with sublime assurance of their ultimate success no longer appeared efficacious, even with good administration. The Indian death rate was exceeding the birth rate, and their economic position was clearly worsening.

When tribal identity became blurred, one of the great objectives of the reformers was accomplished, but the stubborn Indians stoutly refused to become white men. Instead, as their unique tribal characteristics withered away, they replaced them with practices borrowed from other Indians. As with the peyote cult which generated the Native American Church, so with the songs, dances, and handicrafts. Intertribal contacts in the boarding schools and the crowding together of tribes into smaller areas led to a considerable cultural exchange and standardization. Formerly inveterate enemies visited each other's settlements and contributed to the rise of a Pan-Indian movement.

Occasionally the Indians adopted white practices or techniques in a curious fashion. The elaborate pompadour hair style and the long dress of Seminole women is not an ancient tribal custom but rather an adaptation of the Gibson girl style of the turn of the century. Beadwork and weaving designs standardized among other tribes frequently are not the result of native artistic genius but can be traced back to patterns provided by whites seeking a marketable product.

But items of this nature were of small comfort to the reformer or administrator. He could hardly conclude but that the policy of acculturation under duress was a failure. Nor, unless he considered the Indian death rate a solution, could he agree with the Commissioner of Indian Affairs who designated the period around 1917 as "the beginning of the end of the Indian problem."

VI

The Indian New Deal and After

One of the truisms of the history of Franklin Roosevelt's New Deal is that its roots lie far back of 1933. The same thing can certainly be said of the new deal for the red man which is associated with Roosevelt's administration. As mentioned earlier, there were reforms in personnel procurement and the operation of Indian schools around the turn of the century. While they eliminated some of the glaring inequities among the reservations, the changes introduced a new rigidity and centralization of administration. This created a new set of problems in view of the continuing Indian heterogeneity. No general policy, regardless of how carefully conceived or well intended, could be applied fairly to the several hundred Indian societies. The innovations in the field of medical care illustrated this.

A private survey to determine the incidence of tuberculosis among the tribesmen helped focus attention on this calamitous aspect of the Indian problem. By 1910 a medical division had been created within the Indian Service, and Congress had appropriated funds to combat the spread of trachoma, the disease of the eye to which the Indians were particularly susceptible. Although appropriations for medical purposes increased after 1910, the death rate did not begin to decline until about 1930. Some Indians refused to avail themselves of the improved facilities, preferring to rely upon their medicine men and folk remedies. Among tribesmen like the Navahos, who believed that death desecrated a dwelling, there was a tendency to hospitalize only the obviously dying. This practice earned hospitals the reputation of being deathtraps and further discouraged their normal use.

"Health and Sanitation" was one of the topics discussed by the Committee of One Hundred, which the Secretary of the Interior appointed in 1923 after public indignation flared over a plan to divest the Pueblos of land. The committee failed to make any sweeping recommendations for reform, but its activities and the Pueblo case reawakened interest after World War I in the problem of Indian administration. A symposium in a national magazine revealed that while there was no unanimity of opinion on what should be done, there was general discontent with the prevailing situation. It was significant that for the first time a majority, including the ethnologist Frederick Webb Hodge and the journalist Mark Sullivan, deplored the effort to obliterate the unique qualities of Indian culture. A minority, including the veteran Herbert Welsh, reiterated their faith in the traditional civilizing policies, if properly administered.

The principal fruit of the re-examination of government policies was the decision of Secretary of the Interior Herbert

The Indian New Deal and After

Work to request a private concern, the Institute for Government Research, to make a survey and propose a program. Under the direction of Dr. Lewis Meriam and financed by a grant from John D. Rockefeller, Jr., specialists in fields including law, education, and health visited Indian communities throughout the United States. Published in 1928, the Meriam Report provided reformers with badly needed ammunition. It gave priority to medical and school improvements and the creation of a long-range planning division. The report also recommended raising personnel standards in the Indian Service and a much closer scrutiny of proposals for further allotment. Severalty was not repudiated, but it was suggested that "Too much reliance was placed on the sheer effect of individual land ownership and not enough was done to educate the Indians in the use of the land."

Senators caught up in the enthusiasm of the movement began an investigation of their own which ran for several years. Executive branch implementation of any of the recommendations, however, had to await the Hoover administration. To head the Indian Service Herbert Hoover brought in as Commissioner and Assistant Commissioner of Indian Affairs two philanthropists and fellow Quakers, Charles J. Rhoads and J. Henry Scattergood. The President's choice for Secretary of the Interior was Ray Lyman Wilbur, who, in the symposium mentioned above, had expressed a preference for integrating the Indian into American society. To accomplish this within twenty-five years Wilbur proposed a temporary expansion of government services in order to accelerate the movement toward acculturation. But Rhoads and Scattergood were prepared to make haste slowly. They inaugurated surveys which provided the first accurate information about the numbers and condition of the Indian population but altered few major policies.

Their four-year tenure saw the only conspicuous changes made in the area of education. Numerous day schools were founded and subsidies for boarding schools were reduced markedly. Attendance at public schools was encouraged. The total appropriations for the education of Indian youth increased fourfold. Less conspicuous, but important, were moves to improve personnel policies further, and to slow the loss of Indian lands. Even the Board of Indian Commissioners now publicly acknowledged the failure of the severalty program.

Hampering the efforts to improve the Indian's lot was the depression which struck in 1929. Its baneful effects, coupled with drought and grasshoppers, seemed to provide the final crushing blows to the Indian economy. The Red Cross distributed tons of flour among the Indians and the War Department shipped them carloads of surplus clothing. But as a people who even in prosperous times were near the bottom of the economic scale, the Indians suffered severely.

The depression shook the faith of many Americans in the nineteenth-century version of individualism. The hordes of unemployed seemed to demonstrate that we already had too many factory workers and too many farmers. And if the government was forced to succor college-trained white Americans, it was patently absurd to continue to talk of the average reservation Indian moving into a free, competitive society.

Relief measures which established Civilian Conservation Camps for Indians and found other ways of funneling federal money into the reservations were the first order of business for the new Roosevelt administration. But more ambitious

The Indian New Deal and After

plans were in the wind. By 1933 a combination of circumstances had made possible a drastic reorientation of our policies. The Rhoads-Scattergood administration had laid a firm base for reform. The Democrats controlled both the executive and legislative branches which would facilitate adoption of any new program. Congress was mulling over a Senate committee report representing four years' study and calling for major changes in the Indian Service. A President peculiarly receptive to new ideas had appointed as Secretary of the Interior Harold Ickes, who was well acquainted with the Indian problem. Furthermore, John Collier, Roosevelt's choice as Commissioner of Indian Affairs, was a social scientist who had served as an officer of the American Indian Defense Association for ten years. And public opinion was ready for change. In January, 1934, less than a year after Collier took office, representatives of the Indian Rights Association, the General Federation of Women's Clubs, the American Indian Defense Association, the National Council of American Indians, the Indian Committee of the American Civil Liberties Union, and the National Association on Indian Affairs conferred in Washington. Encouraged by Collier, they adopted a resolution calling for repudiation of the severalty policy and the vigorous promotion of "community ownership and control."

The Meriam Report had suggested exploring the possibilities of corporate ownership, and Collier indorsed it as a means of preserving Indian societies. In his first annual report the new commissioner outlined the policies he proposed to pursue. Not only should allotment be abandoned, but allotted lands should be consolidated for tribal use. Financial aid should be made available to co-operative Indian groups, and they should be instructed in the latest methods of land use. The trend away

155

from boarding schools should be accelerated and the day schools be employed as a means of improving community welfare through work with the adults as well as the children. More Indians should be brought into the Indian Service and more self-government encouraged among Indian societies. As a corollary to this, the Indian Service should be decentralized and local officials given more latitude in dealing with the problems of their charges.

Flora Seymour, a staunch advocate of the old integration policies, denounced Collier's approach as "a unique program of regimentation, which in several basic features is the most extreme gesture yet made by the administration toward a Communistic experiment." Other critics were to be found among missionary groups alarmed at Collier's intention to invoke the Indian's constitutional right to his native religion. But these were exceptions. Most agreed with Roosevelt's declaration that the time had come to "extend to the Indian the fundamental rights of political liberty and local self-government and the opportunities of education and economic assistance that they require in order to attain a wholesome American life." In June, 1934, the President signed the Wheeler-Howard (Indian Reorganization) Act giving legislative sanction to the new policies. Indicative of the new approach was the fact that the legislation did not force the changes on the tribes but rather permitted them to take advantage of the terms if they so desired.

One of Collier's basic assumptions with reference to the Indian had been: "Clan instinct, clan operation of assets, is inherent in him. The tribal Indian remains the self-reliant and self-supporting Indian." The Wheeler-Howard Act reflected this in its provisions for tribal constitutions and business corporations, and in its land policy. The allotment acts were repealed, the trust period continued indefinitely, and the unsold lands remaining after allotment were to be returned to the Indians. There was also a provision for the purchase of new land for the tribesmen and soon over a million acres had been acquired at a cost to the government of nearly $4,000,000. In addition, a revolving fund was created to provide credit for Indian agricultural and industrial projects.

The Wheeler-Howard Act also expanded educational opportunities for the Indian by improving facilities and establishing loan funds from which individual students might borrow. By altering the job qualifications, preference was given to Indian applicants for positions with the Indian Service. This, coupled with the emphasis on local as opposed to Washington control, served to provide a service more responsive to the needs of the tribesmen.

There were the customary wide variations in the Indian reaction to the new legislation. Some of the Oklahoma Indians who had integrated successfully opposed the Wheeler-Howard Act as a perpetuation of an inferior status. While over a hundred tribes chose to draw up constitutions and twice that many economic organizations were chartered, it was soon apparent that unfamiliarity with American political and economic organizations and practices nullified the efforts of some. Better received were the new policies which condoned if not encouraged native religions, ceremonials, and crafts. But so long had repressive policies been in effect that some of the practices were beyond revival. What frequently appeared was a blend of tribal remnants and borrowings from other Indians. The results helped further the Pan-Indian movement and had an incalculable effect in raising Indian morale by removing the stigma previously associated with tribal cultures.

Obvious to all was the extent to which the relief projects and the new policies were remaking the face of Indian land. The old acres and the nearly 3,000,000 added by 1940 benefited from the work of the experts who devised plans to irrigate the dry lands and drain the wet, resod eroded soil, plant trees, and construct roads. Other experts worked to improve the quality of the Indian herds and reduce the number of livestock to a figure the range could properly support.

The continuing improvement in medical services was reflected in the steadily declining death rate after 1930. This decline was principally responsible for the slow increase in the Indian population. A sounder financial situation stemmed from the flow of federal funds to the reservations—$70,000,000 in relief funds alone in the first three years of the New Deal—and the increased productivity of Indian farms and ranches. John Collier estimated that in the first twenty years of the Wheeler-Howard Act beef production went up 2,300 per cent and farm production climbed 400 per cent. One incidental effect of the improved financial situation of the Indians was, paradoxically, a weakening of the tribal ties which Collier's policies had otherwise strengthened. With money in their pockets some Indians were beginning to develop the self-interest which detracted from clan and family unity.

The impact of World War II on the Indians produced a similar effect. Subject to the draft now, about 25,000 Indians served in the armed forces. Nearly twice as many were drawn from the reservations by industry as the flow of federal relief funds dried up. For those tribes with a warrior tradition the rate of enlistment was high, and the volunteers enjoyed considerable status with their fellows. Even though their military service might be limited to clerical duty in a quartermaster depot, they were accorded the respect fighting men had traditionally held in their society. Among those few tribes which had been peaceful, there was a significant lack of enthusiasm for the war effort. In one tribe, long vacant offices in religious organizations were filled by youths seeking exemption from military service.

Wartime incomes and experience accelerated the detribalization process. The mechanics of the allotment system for dependents of service personnel impressed the virtues of monogamy on Indians who had failed to observe them before. Torn between the old beliefs and their pride in their armed forces personnel, the Navahos overcame the horror of the dead to accord their casualties heroes' burials.

The returned veterans also did their part to hasten the end of the old way of life. Tribal leaders found them less amenable. Government officials heard bitter complaints against the federal law prohibiting the sale of liquor to Indians and the discrimination of some western states against Indian voters. Two suits in which the Bureau of Indian Affairs had a hand removed Arizona's and New Mexico's ban on voting for off-reservation and literate Indians, ending the last vestiges of official discrimination. Growing Indian awareness of the value of the ballot is seen in the 1959 annual meeting of the National Congress of American Indians which had political action as its theme. Representatives of seventy tribes heard speakers advise them to "Participate in the political party of your choice." Experts also lectured on the necessity for good public relations and urged the tribal representatives to overcome traditional reticence and present their case forcibly. That they are beginning to do so is evidenced by the attention Indian voters are now getting from office-seekers. Even more impressive is the appearance of Indians as candidates for public office.

Equality in drinking was achieved in 1953 by an act of Congress which removed the ban on off-reservation liquor sales to Indians and approved local option for reservations. Alcoholism has always been a major problem for Indians, and there is no evidence that the new policy ameliorated it. Infrequently a case like that of Ira Hayes, a Pima and one of the marines who became famous through the flag-raising on Mount Suribachi, attracts national attention. But for every Hayes whose chronic alcoholism attracted national attention, there are hundreds who degenerate with less publicity. Gallup, New Mexico, "The Indian Capital," sees scores of Indians arrested every weekend for difficulties growing out of excessive drinking. The stock explanations for the high rate of alcoholism—inadequate recreational facilities, lack of parental supervision, and escapism—don't suggest any improvement in the situation in the near future.

The removal of the ban on off-reservation liquor sales to Indians was a minor action in a drive to "emancipate" the Indian, and, to use Senator Watkins' expression, get "the government out of the Indian business." Proposals to integrate the Indian into American society were hardly new. Beginning with George Washington's administration, this had been the announced objective. Even John Collier justified requests for additional appropriations in 1944 by the same rationalization employed in the Rhoads-Scattergood regime—spend more now in order to speed the day the Bureau of Indian Affairs might be inactivated. Indeed, the Johnson-O'Malley Act, which Congress passed shortly before the Wheeler-Howard Act, provided for the shifting of some of the responsibility for Indian education to state and local governments.

By 1940 some of the enthusiasm for the Wheeler-Howard Act had dissipated. Despite the expenditure of millions of dollars an Indian problem remained. As World War II defense expenditures mounted, the Indian budget was slashed. In Congress there was talk of abolishing the Bureau of Indian Affairs and even repealing the Wheeler-Howard Act. The return of peace did not end the agitation. The Hoover Commission, which made recommendations in 1949 for the reorganization of the government, advocated the transfer to state governments of social programs for the Indian. The commission also urged policies which would encourage and assist Indians to leave the reservation and enter the mainstream of American life.

Dillon S. Myer, who became Commissioner of Indian Affairs in 1950, heartily indorsed the new "termination" policy. During his administration the Wheeler-Howard Act was not repealed, but it was gutted. The revolving loan fund, for example, was not liquidated—in 1952 the Bureau of Indian Affairs simply stopped making loans from it. Wherever possible, health and education responsibilities were shifted to state and local governments to be aided by subsidies from Washington.

The Eisenhower administration rode to power, in part, on a pledge to diminish the role of the federal government. It speedily learned that in practice it was difficult to find an area where withdrawal of federal services did not evoke anguished outcries from potent pressure groups. The relatively inarticulate Indians were thus the recipient of much of this attention. The Eighty-second Congress passed one bill and a concurrent resolution which indicated its solicitude for termination. The bill provided for the transfer to five states of responsibility for law and order among their Indians and opened the door for similar action by other states. The President signed the measure reluctantly. He might well have vetoed it, since it ignored any wishes the Indians might have in the matter and could eviscerate any law enforcement programs they might have evolved under the Wheeler-Howard Act. The other action, the concurrent resolution, was a sweeping statement of the termination policy and called on the Secretary of the Interior to suggest legislation to end the connection of several tribes with the federal government.

The following session of Congress saw ten termination bills presented and six passed. And in 1955 the health program of the Indian Bureau was transferred to the public health service. Obviously this action did not end the federal government's responsibility in the matter, but it did further the policy of termination by removing Indian health programs from a special category and merging them with those of the general population.

The ardor for termination was subsiding by 1956. Some had advocated it as leading to "greater freedom and responsibility" for the Indians, and as an antidote to the Wheeler-Howard Act's perpetuation of race-consciousness. These observers tended to equate a policy fostering sand painting and basket weaving with illiteracy and a high mortality rate. But among those who had worked the longest with the red man and had contributed their knowledge and interest to the Indian welfare organizations were many strident critics of termination. A few hinted that oil and timber were the real motives behind some termination plans and the record of the whites since

State Historical Society of North Dakota

Fort Yates Boarding School kitchen (photograph by Frank Fisk, about 1900)

Blackfoot Reservation home, 1951

Smithsonian Institution

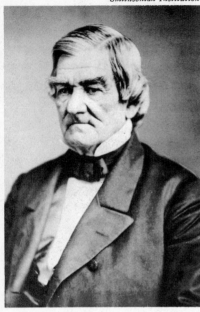

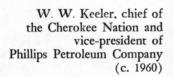

John Ross (1790–1866),
of the Cherokee tribe
(photograph by A. Z.
Shindler, 1858).

W. W. Keeler, chief of
the Cherokee Nation and
vice-president of
Phillips Petroleum Company
(c. 1960)

1492 made this a logical surmise.

The chorus of criticism of the government's policies brought disclaimers from officials culminating ultimately in a public statement by Secretary of the Interior Seaton in 1958. While defending termination in general, he made it clear that it would be implemented only after those to whom it was to be applied thoroughly understood and accepted it. This, coupled with the Secretary's denunciation as "incredible, even criminal" the withdrawal of government protection and services before the Indians were capable of fending for themselves, stilled most of the clamor. However, had the friends of the red man not been so vociferous, Indians might have been "emancipated" who were as poorly equipped for the transition as those Seminoles who spoke no English and who lived by hunting and fishing.

Perhaps 10,000 Indians had their ties with the federal government severed during the heyday of termination. For those like the Alabama-Coushatta in Texas it was relatively painless because the state assumed the federal government's responsibilities. For tribes like the Menominee and Klamath it has proved to be a much more complicated operation. In both instances the time limit had to be extended and modifications made in the original plan.

An official of Wisconsin testified that the state was caught with no plans for the assumption of responsibility for the Menominees. The solution finally agreed upon provided that the reservation be transformed into a new county in Wisconsin and that a corporation be chartered to handle Menominee tribal assets.

Similar, in that timber resources were involved here also, was the Klamath situation. Concern was expressed about the impact that a forced sale of tribal holdings would have on the Oregon lumber market, a waterfowl refuge, and the Klamath themselves. One of the tribesmen said that the anticipated per capita distributions of nearly $50,000 to each Indian would be "like throwing a steak to the dogs. Too few of us are prepared."

Termination was a rugged experience for both tribes. Overnight, Menominee County came into being with a multitude of problems. The median income for the county was about half that for the rest of Wisconsin, while the birth rate was double—a formula for poverty if there ever was one. The tribal corporation had to employ white managers, and sometimes their solutions to the tribe's financial problems, for example, leasing sites for vacation homes to whites, aroused Menominee ire. One faction of the tribe, headed by Ada Deer, began to lobby for repeal of termination. Late in 1973 Congress reversed itself, and the Menominee again became wards of the Federal Government.

Unlike the Menominee termination, that of the Klamath resulted in the breakup of tribal holdings. In 1961 most Klamath elected to withdraw from the tribe, receiving $43,500 per capita shares in the process. Many of them chose to take it in cash, providing the national press with feature stories about Indians wandering around with small fortunes in paper bags and engaging in orgies of spending. Those Klamath who chose to remain affiliated with the tribe and hold their property in common had it managed for them by a bank. Dissatisfaction with the bank's performance was a factor in deciding the remaining tribal members in 1969 to dissolve the tribe as a business entity and to distribute its assets, providing $103,000 per capita shares.

By 1960 termination had few public advocates, as manifested

by its repudiation by both presidential candidates that year. Nevertheless, certain basic problems remained unsolved. Most speakers addressing themselves to the Indian condition began their talks with a dismal litany of infant mortality rates, unemployment statistics, and substandard housing and medical care. Comparing the Indian standard of living with that afforded by the most highly industrialized society in the world only made the portrayal bleaker.

Two proposals to ameliorate the situation were to relocate Indians to urban areas, where they could find better employment opportunities, and to encourage light industry and tourism on the reservations. The government's relocation program subsidized the movement of both individuals and families who volunteered to go to selected urban areas. The subsidy generally covered transportation from the reservation and the initial expense of relocating, including food, housing, and vocational training. Of those relocated, some proved incapable of supporting themselves and ended up on relief rolls, and at least one-third returned to the reservation. As long as ties with the reservation existed, relocated Indians who encountered difficulty adjusting had that alternative. Dumping the reservation's surplus populations on urban relief agencies, therefore, clearly constituted no solution. That Commissioner Dillon S. Myer, whose name was most closely associated with relocation, had administered to relocated Japanese in World War II was further reason to damn the program.

Indian critics of relocation also attacked it as cultural genocide, a new tactic in the centuries-long attack on Indian societies. They urged that, rather than trying to take the tribesmen to the jobs, jobs should be taken to the tribesmen by the encouragement of light industry and tourism on and near reservations.

By the mid-1960's self-determination had replaced termination as the goal of government policy. Self-determination, interpreted both economically and politically, had at least the rhetorical support of White House incumbents. Lyndon Johnson said, "We must affirm the right of the first Americans to remain Indians . . . [and] their right to freedom of choice and self-determination." President Nixon reassured the Indians by saying, "And we must make clear that Indians can become independent of Federal control without being cut off from Federal concern and Federal support."

Federal financial support for Indians has grown markedly since 1960. By the mid-1970's Indian programs and their administration cost approximately a billion dollars a year, with the Bureau of Indian Affairs accounting for only about half of the total. The biggest increases came as a result of the new programs initiated by the Johnson administration's war on poverty. As the most depressed minority in the nation, Indians clearly would, and did, command the attention of a government dedicated to ending poverty in the United States. Since the mid-1960's federal money has been available as never before to upgrade Indian housing, stimulate local industry, improve Indian education, and in many other ways better the quality of Indian life.

The results have not been uniformly beneficial, some of the programs and projects being poorly planned. Moreover, a former Sioux tribal chairman has deplored the corrupting influence of the federal largesse on Indian tribal governments. There have been embarrassingly frequent incidents of malfeasance in office.

The Indian New Deal and After

More significant has been the failure of the efforts to produce substantial employment for Indians on and near reservations through attraction of light industry and the development of tourism. The government still employs more of that population than does private industry. With hundreds of communities across the country competing for any new factory, reservations have had little success in attracting other than marginal industries to the subsidies they can enjoy in the first few years on a reservation. Nor should this be unexpected. Few reservations offer the combination of a pool of trained workers, adequate transportation facilities, and access to markets sought by industrialists.

Tourism would appear to have more potential, with the government subsidizing the development of resorts by low-interest loans and outright grants, as it has on many reservations. However, if these resorts are to provide employment for local Indians as well as income for tribal coffers, a reorientation of traditional work habits may be required. To be successful in resort operation and thereby provide a base for ameliorating their serious unemployment, housing shortage, and related problems, Indians must develop the skills and work ethic that are found among successful resort operators elsewhere. The same may by said for light industry, where the adaptability of a work force to assembly-line production methods and fifty-week-a-year work schedules can make the difference between success or failure of a business. It would appear to be difficult for many Indians to enjoy the standard of living provided by an industrial society without losing some of the independence and individuality that are the most admired features of their cultures.

Casual talk about economic self-determination for tribes also ignores certain realities. With the exception of the Navajo, and perhaps a half dozen others, the tribes do not have the population or land base to aspire to any real degree of economic independence. The average tribe has little land and numbers fewer than four thousand people, among them many who no longer reside in the tribal area.

A potential source of capital for tribal economic development has existed since 1946. At that time Congress created the Indian Claims Commission to expedite termination. By 1978 the commission had awarded judgments against the United States totaling over half a billion dollars. These awards stem from injustices perpetrated by the government in earlier transactions, particularly acquisitions of Indian land. Although Congress must approve tribal proposals for use of the awards, the Indians can devote them to tribal economic development as well as per capita distributions.

The land claims of Alaskan natives (Indians, Eskimos, Aleuts) were settled by Congress without reference to the Indian Claims Commission. As late as 1960 the claims of the Alaskan natives, which were intact when the United States purchased the territory, had been uncompromised by treaty or other agreement. This situation might have lasted indefinitely had it not been necessary to clear the way for the Alaskan pipeline. In 1971 Congress legislated a settlement that guaranteed the Alaskan natives title to forty million acres and would ultimately pay them nearly one billion dollars. They appear to have acquired a real base for economic and political self-determination.

The Indians of the contiguous forty-eight states clearly are not in so advantageous a position as the Alaskan natives. While aspiring to self-determination, many in fact are becoming more dependent on the Federal Government. Since the mid-1960's, Indian groups, particularly in the East, that had lost or never had federal recognition have succeeded in obtaining it. Indeed, one of the national associations concerned with Indians prides itself on having assisted a small tribe of 250 people to acquire 15 acres of land which could help qualify the tribe for federal recognition. The principal benefit of such recognition is eligibility for the services and subsidies the government makes available to Indian groups. As one Indian put it, the Federal Government has become their new buffalo.

If in recent years Indians have become more dependent on government subsidy, at least in principle they have achieved a greater degree of political self-determination. They have sought, and the government has granted them, a larger role in controlling their own destinies. The most significant development in this direction was the Indian Self-Determination and Education Assistance Act of 1975, which authorizes tribes to contract with the government to perform, at government expense, services previously performed by government employees. This is in line with the objective of self-determination: Indians directing their own destinies while preserving their special rights and wardship status with the Federal Government.

A new generation of Indian leaders has helped bring about this new government policy and is ready to implement it. Frequently college trained themselves, they can draw upon a growing cadre of Indian graduates in law and business to advise and aid them. Articulate and familiar with the political system, these Native Americans no longer are content to permit Congress or the Bureau of Indian Affairs to unilaterally declare and implement policy. Unlike the situation as late as 1965, it is inconceivable today that major Indian legislation would be proposed without thorough consultation with tribesmen. Likewise, it is inconceivable today that Indians should not be in top positions in the Bureau of Indian Affairs, although only one Native American held the position of Commissioner of Indian Affairs before 1966. When President Carter, in 1977, created the position of Assistant Secretary of Indian Affairs to replace the post of Commissioner of Indian Affairs, it seemed only proper that he appoint a tribal member, Forrest J. Girard, to the new position.

The same trend is apparent in the national associations which have been the principal spokesmen for Indians for a century. Until recently these were run exclusively by white people, with only an occasional Indian on stage at an annual meeting. However, in the last few years, tribesmen have been brought in to top positions in these organizations.

The contributions of the Red Power movement to Indian self-determination are significant. In the popular mind Red Power is associated most often with the confrontations beginning in the early 1960's and peaking ten years later. It actually dates back at least to the founding of the National Congress of American Indians (NCAI) in 1944, and probably to the early Pan-Indian movements, most important of which was the Society of American Indians founded in 1911. Although they differed on objectives, these early organizations were the initial all-Indian efforts to have a voice in their future. Red Power's objective was best summarized in 1966 by Vine Deloria, Jr., then Executive Director of NCAI: "Red Power means we want power over our own lives. . . . We simply want the power, the political and economic power, to run our own lives in our own way."

Three organizations have been most visible in the Red Power

Dennis Banks, Chippewa, 1972
N.E.W.S. photo

Russell Means, Sioux, 1972
N.E.WS. photo

Indians occupying Bureau of Indian Affairs, November 1972
N.E.W.S. photo

movement, the NCAI, the National Indian Youth Council (NIYC), and the American Indian Movement (AIM). The NCAI has been described as the organization for Indian radicals over thirty. The NIYC was created in 1961 by younger Indians who had been attracted as uninvited observers to Professor Sol Tax's American Indian Chicago Conference, which had close ties with the NCAI. AIM originated with Chippewas living in Minneapolis-St. Paul and became the spokesman particularly of the urban Indians seeking the same services the government made available to Indians on and near reservations.

But Red Power was not confined to formal organizations. It also found expression in individuals like Mad Bear Anderson, the Tuscarora, and groups like the one that seized control of Alcatraz Island in 1969 and held it for nineteen months.

While NCAI members like Vine Deloria, Jr., and D'Arcy McNickle helped formulate the philosophical basis for Red Power, the headlines went to those Indians like Mad Bear Anderson, Russell Means, and Dennis Banks, the latter two AIM leaders who commanded attention by leading demonstrations and issuing militant statements.

That Indian protest took the character it did in the 1960's and early 1970's is not surprising. American society in that era already had spawned black and campus militants, and the red variety clearly was indebted to them for much of its rhetoric and tactics. Likewise, the cycle of Indian activism seemed to fit a pattern similar to that of black and campus militants. Their early demonstrations attracted thorough coverage by the press and considerable interest and sympathy in the general population. But the public's interest waned as the novelty wore off. Also, those non-Indians who had been amused or sympathetic when Plymouth Rock or Mount Rushmore were taken over peaceably by Red Power activists, became alarmed at the violence and property destruction associated with the occupation of the Bureau of Indian Affairs in November, 1972, and the hamlet of Wounded Knee a few months later. Indians might protest that they were acting purely in self-defense, but the shift in public opinion—a white backlash—suggests that such confrontations had become counter-productive, particularly for a people increasingly dependent upon the good will of Congress.

The militants, harassed by law enforcement agents and expensive and time-consuming court actions, seemed to have subsided by the late 1970's. However, they could claim some responsibility for having sensitized the general public to anti-Indian racial slurs and practices. And older and more conservative Indian leaders had learned that the implied threat to invite AIM to assist them could be another tool in bargaining with government officials. On the positive side, the militants had given many Indians a sense of pride in being Indian, as is evidenced in the considerable increase between 1960 and 1970 in those declaring themselves Indian for census purposes. This heightened racial pride was fed by a spate of new Indian publications like *Akwesasne Notes, Wasaja,* and *The Indian Historian.* It was manifested, among other ways, in strenuous protests against adoption policies which contribute to the destruction of Indian families.

As the nation prepares to enter the 1980's and its water and energy problems intensify, it is clear that Indian leadership is coming of age none too soon. The rapid growth of population in the arid West has brought new pressures on Indian water rights. Constant vigilance and knowledge of how the legal system works—and can be worked—are absolutely essential if Indians are to save the water upon which, in many cases, their continued existence as Indians depends. Similarly, if tribes are to derive maximum benefit from the coal and oil deposits beneath their land, their leaders must be able not only to recognize tribal interests but to protect them. The appearance of the Native American Rights Fund, with private foundation assistance, and the emergence of Indian law centers at the University of New Mexico and the University of Oklahoma testify to a growing competence in this area.

Two landmark decisions suggest a new day for the Indian in the federal courts. In 1974 a judge ruled that tribesmen in Washington State were entitled to catch up to fifty percent of the salmon and steelhead trout in fishing off their reservations, opening the door to renewal of tribal claims to territory outside their current holdings. In the other case, the Passamaquoddy and Penobscot tribes of Maine have been rejuvenated by a court decision requiring the Federal Government to represent them in suits to nullify land cessions to states made without the supervision of the Federal Government. This could mean eastern tribes regaining hundreds of thousands of acres, plus substantial cash settlements. Clearly the dangers to Indian interests are still great, but so are the opportunities for overcoming them.

The Indian problem is complex today, but not as complex as it was in the early days of the republic. Tribal armed might and foreign intervention complicated all discussion of the problem then. Today the red men are one of the minorities in our population, perhaps on the average the most impoverished and poorest prepared of all our minority groups. Although hampered by race prejudice in some areas, in others the Indian classification is a defense against the discrimination their dark-skinned neighbors suffer. Particularly in the eastern United States there are to be found small groups of mixed white-Indian-Negro ancestry who cling to their Indian title when they have long since lost all vestiges of their aboriginal culture.

That such an individual is considered in the same category as the fullblood, non–English-speaking Indian of the Southwest, of whom there are thousands, is evidence that diversity is still the principal stumbling block in the formulation of policy for the Indian population. Jet pilots and petroleum company vice-presidents are proud of their Indian ancestry. But so are illiterate backwoodsmen in North Carolina. And among the Indian inhabitants of a single community, Yankton, South Dakota, scholars have distinguished at least four different levels of acculturation. Further testimony to this diversity is to be found in the more than one hundred Indian languages spoken in the mid-twentieth century.

As in the days of Columbus, the variety of Indians seems infinite. Obviously, maximum flexibility is indispensable in policy formulation and the interpretation of the more than five thousand statutes and treaties. And in simple justice to people whom we have looted and oppressed in the past, theirs should be the ultimate decision in all discussions of their future. That, however, is unlikely if tribes remain economically dependent on Congress, whose members will control the purse strings.

Although total assimilation seems even farther away than it did twenty years ago, Indians already have contributed much to a composite culture. Monongahela, Wisconsin, Appalachian, and hundreds of others bear witness to the white practice of adopting Indian place names. Were it not for the Indian we could not denounce Tammany, drink hooch, caucus, or bury

The Indian New Deal and After

the hatchet. Like our vocabulary, our diet has been enriched by Indian offerings since the days the Pilgrims were introduced to planked shad and the clambake. Sweet potatoes, peanuts, pumpkins, maize, and tobacco have nourished and consoled us. We have found relief in pharmaceuticals the Indian discovered for us, followed the routes across the continent he first charted, and subdued the land with practices borrowed from him we were dispossessing.

If a society's treatment of its minorities is an index of its character, Indian–United States relations are a gold mine for the social historian. In our image of and plans for the Indian, whether it be in the religion-saturated seventeenth century, the halcyon days of rugged individualism of the nineteenth century, or the welfare statism of the 1930's, will be found an excellent mirror of our own ideals and aspirations. That our record is poor is not to be denied. But we may take what comfort we can from the knowledge that what resulted from the clash of cultures here is not drastically different from what has occurred elsewhere. The Japanese are still trying to assimilate their native race, the Ainu; reports from Brazil's interior sound like those from the Great Plains in the 1870's; Australians are futilely trying to impart the virtues of private property to New Guinea tribesmen. For Australia's own aboriginal population, opinion is being expressed that to deny them equality would be "un-Christian, undemocratic, and un-Australian." Such a familiar theme should dispel any idea that our situation is unique.

Important Dates

1622	Opechancanough's first uprising in Virginia
1637	Pequot War in New England
1644	Opechancanough's last uprising in Virginia
1672–76	King Philip's War ends organized resistance of southern New England tribes
1689–97	King William's War
1702–13	Queen Anne's War
1711–12	Tuscarora War
1715–16	Yamasee War
1722	Abenaki War
1744–48	King George's War
1754	Albany Conference
1754–63	French and Indian War
1763	Pontiac's Conspiracy
1763	Proclamation of 1763 restricts westward movement of settlers
1764	English revise administration of Indian Affairs
1774	Lord Dunmore's War
1775–83	American Revolution
1775	Continental Congress assumes responsibility for Indian affairs
1790	McGillivray's Treaty of New York
1790	Indians defeat Harmar
1791	Indians defeat St. Clair

Important Dates

1794	Battle of Fallen Timbers, August 20
1795	Treaty of Greenville
1796–1822	Government factory system in operation
1811	Battle of Tippecanoe, November 7
1812–16	War of 1812
1813–14	Creek War
1816	Licenses in the Indian trade restricted to American citizens
1819	Fund created by Congress for civilizing the Indians
1824	Bureau of Indian Affairs established
1830	Removal Bill
1831	*Cherokee Nation* vs. *Georgia*
1832	*Worcester* vs. *Georgia*
1832	Office of Commissioner of Indian Affairs created
1834	Indian Trade and Intercourse Act redefines Indian country
	Indian Reorganization Act introduces changes in the Indian Service
1835–42	Seminole War
1846	Texas Indian tribes come under federal control
1848	Treaty of Guadalupe Hidalgo brings additional tribes under United States jurisdiction
1849	Office of Indian Affairs transferred to Interior Department
1861–65	Civil War
1862	Minnesota Sioux Uprising
1863–64	Kit Carson campaigns against the Navahos and Apaches
1864	Sand Creek Massacre, November 28
1866	Fetterman Massacre on the Bozeman Trail, December 21
1867	Board of Indian Commissioners established
1867	Peace Commission blames whites for plains troubles
1869	Grant's Quaker policy inaugurated
1870	Congress appropriates first sum specifically for Indian education
1871	Treaty process abandoned
1872–73	Modoc War
1874–75	Red River War
1876	Custer Massacre, June 26

American Indians

1877	Chief Joseph leads Nez Percé outbreak
1878	Congress appropriates first funds for Indian police
1879	Ute War
1879	Captain Richard H. Pratt founds Carlisle Indian School
1882	Indian Rights Association founded
1883	First Mohonk Conference held
1883	Courts of Indian Offences inaugurated
1885	Publication of Helen Jackson's *A Century of Dishonor*
1885	Last buffalo herd exterminated
1886	Geronimo surrenders, ending Apache resistance
1887	Dawes Severalty Act
1890–91	Ghost Dance movement
1890	Massacre at Wounded Knee, December 29
1907	Burke Act amends the Dawes Severalty Act
1910	Medical division established within the Indian Service
1923	Committee of One Hundred surveys the Indian problem
1924	Congress grants citizenship to all Indians
1928	Meriam Report published
1934	Wheeler-Howard (Indian Reorganization) Act
1944	National Congress of American Indians founded
1946	Congress creates Indian Claims Commission
1949	Hoover Commission recommends termination
1953	Congress revises Indian liquor laws
1958	Secretary of Interior Seaton modifies termination policy
1968	American Indian Movement founded
1969	Indians occupy Alcatraz Island
1971	Congress settles Alaskan native claims
1972	Indians occupy Bureau of Indian Affairs headquarters
1973	Armed confrontation at Wounded Knee, South Dakota
1975	Indian Self-Determination and Education Assistance Act
1978	Position of Assistant Secretary of Interior for Indian Affairs created

Suggested Reading

Since the publication of the first edition of this book in 1961, there has been a marked increase in interest in the history of the Native American. Many useful works have appeared and a selection has been made from them to produce this revised bibliography.

Two indispensable bibliographies are George Peter Murdock and Timothy J. O'Leary, *Ethnographic Bibliography of North America* (5 vols., 1975), and Francis Paul Prucha, *A Bibliographical Guide to the History of Indian-White Relations in the United States* (1977).

For the student, the best introduction to Indian culture is Harold E. Driver, *Indians of North America* (1969). Muriel H. Wright, *A Guide to the Indian Tribes of Oklahoma* (1951), contains excellent sketches of sixty-five tribes.

Among the works which have surveyed the entire period of Indian-white relations, the most recent and best is Wilcomb E. Washburn, *The Indian in America* (1975). Angie Debo, *A History of the Indians of the United States,* is also valuable, particularly on the Five Civilized Tribes. A competent survey of United States' policy is to be found in S. Lyman Tyler, *A History of Indian Policy* (1973).

Felix S. Cohen, *Handbook of Federal Indian Law* (1941), contains digests of thousands of treaties and statutes as well as concise historical summaries. For treaties and land cessions, the standard

American Indians

authorities are Charles J. Kappler, *Indian Affairs: Laws and Treaties* (1904), and C. C. Royce, *Indian Land Cessions in the United States,* Bureau of American Ethnology's eighteenth annual report (1899).

Virgil J. Vogel, *American Indian Medicine* (1970), is the most thorough treatment of a complex subject. Henry F. Dobyns has addressed himself to a related and highly controversial topic in *Native American Historical Demography: A Critical Bibliography* (1976).

CHAPTER I

Wilcomb E. Washburn, *Red Man's Land—White Man's Law* (1971), provides a convenient summary of the philosophical basis for early European policies toward Indians, as well as subsequent developments. Imre Sutton, *Indian Land Tenure* (1975), is a valuable survey of the subject and includes a guide to the literature.

For the Southwest, Edward H. Spicer's fine *Cycles of Conquest* (1962) can now be supplemented by Elizabeth A. H. John, *Storms Brewed in Other Men's Worlds* (1975), which includes Texas tribes but is oriented more toward Spanish policy than its impact on the Indians.

Alden Vaughan, *New England Frontier* (1965), traces Puritan-Indian relations to 1675 and concludes that the Puritans have been maligned. Francis Jennings effectively disputes this in *The Invasion of America* (1975) and castigates other white invaders as well. Douglas Edward Leach, who comes closer to Vaughan's than Jenning's viewpoint, is the author of two useful volumes, *Flintlock and Tomahawk: New England in King Philips' War* (1958) and *The Northern Colonial Frontier 1607–1763* (1966). Harold H. Peckham, *The Colonial Wars, 1689–1762* (1964), is a useful summary for their effects on all sections.

The impact of the fur trade and colonization on the Indians of New York can be traced in Van Cleaf Bachman, *Peltries or Plantations* (1969), Thomas Elliot Norton, *The Fur Trade in Colonial New York, 1686–1776* (1974), and Georgiana C. Nammack, *Fraud, Politics and the Dispossession of the Indians* (1969). Allen W. Trelease, *Indian Affairs in Colonial New York* (1960), is still the best book for the seventeenth century. The important role of Wil-

Suggested Reading

liam Johnson can be traced in James Thomas Flexner, *Mohawk Baronet* (1959), and Milton W. Hamilton's more recent and detailed *Sir William Johnson* (1976), which only carries the story to 1763.

Anthony F. C. Wallace, *King of the Delawares: Teedyuscung, 1700–1763* (1949), is a model study of an important figure. C. A. Weslager, *The Delaware Indians* (1972), is a history of that tribe.

Howard W. Peckham, *Pontiac and the Indian Uprising* (1947), is the standard work on that subject. Wilbur R. Jacobs, *Diplomacy and Indian Gifts* (1950), and Randolph C. Downs, *Council Fires on the Upper Ohio* (1940), are invaluable for an understanding of the period.

Verner W. Crane, *The Southern Frontier, 1670–1732* (1928), and David H. Corkran's two volumes, *The Creek Frontier, 1540–1783* (1967), and The Cherokee Frontier (1962), are good for that section's Indian-white relations.

CHAPTER II

The general setting for the Indian role in the Revolution is ably presented in Jack M. Sosin, *The Revolutionary Frontier, 1763–1783* (1967); Barbara Graymont, *The Iroquois in the American Revolution* (1972), is excellent on that subject. *Southern Indians in the American Revolution* (1973), by James H. O'Donnell, III, is brief but effective.

Reginald Horsman, *Expansion and American Indian Policy, 1783–1812* (1967), traces the evolution of policy and the machinery for implementing it. *Seeds of Extinction* (1973), by Bernard W. Sheehan, is the best treatment of the intellectual background for Jeffersonian Indian policy. For the application of that policy to southern tribesmen, and their reaction, see Merritt B. Pound, *Benjamin Hawkins–Indian Agent* (1915); John Walton Caughey, *McGillivray of the Creeks* (1938), and J. Leitch Wright, Jr., *William Augustus Bowles: Director of the Creek Nation* (1967).

For a northern tribe, the previously cited C. A. Weslager, *The Delaware Indians*, is useful for this period as well. A really outstanding volume is Anthony F. C. Wallace, *The Death and Rebirth of the Seneca* (1969). Glen Tucker, *Tecumseh* (1956), is the fullest treatment of that significant figure. Francis Paul Prucha, *The Sword of the Republic: The United States Army on the Frontier, 1783–1846* (1969), traces the military operations of the period.

CHAPTER III

For this period, Prucha's *The Sword of the Republic* is again useful. His *American Indian Policy in the Formative Years: The Indian Trade and Intercourse Acts, 1790–1834* (1962), is a standard reference. It can be supplemented by two valuable recent publications, Herman J. Viola, *Thomas L. McKenney* (1974), the biography of a key figure in the shaping of Indian policy, 1816–1830, and Ronald N. Satz, *American Indian Policy in the Jacksonian Era* (1975).

The removal of the Five Civilized Tribes has attracted the attention of a number of writers. One of the best general treatments is Dale Van Every, *Disinherited* (1966). An unusual approach to the Cherokee story, in that it does credit to those who concluded that prolonged resistance to removal was a mistake, is Thurman Wilkins, *Cherokee Tragedy* (1970). The travail of the Choctaws can be followed in Arthur H. De Rosier, Jr., *The Removal of the Choctaw Indians* (1970), and the career of a Choctaw leader during and after removal is skillfully depicted in W. David Baird, *Peter Pitchlynn* (1972). For a revealing account of the land factor which motivated most support for removal, see Mary Elizabeth Young, *Redskins, Ruffleshirts and Rednecks: Indian Allotments in Alabama and Mississippi, 1830–1860.*

The removal of the Midwestern tribes has received much less attention. Grant Foreman summarizes it in *The Last Trek of the Indians* (1946), and my *The Sac and Fox Indians* (1958) deals with the removal experience of those Indians. *Black Hawk: An Autobiography* (1955), edited by Donald Jackson, is that unusual item, an autobiography of an early nineteenth-century Indian.

Robert F. Berkhofer, Jr., *Salvation and the Savage: An Analysis of Protestant Missions and American Indian Response, 1787–1862* (1965), is excellent. For the work of a Baptist missionary who also had an important role in removal, see George A. Schultz, *An Indian Canaan: Isaac McCoy and the Vision of an Indian State* (1972).

Suggested Reading

CHAPTER IV

To trace Indian policy in the years immediately following the Mexican War, when the United States was invading the Southwest, see Robert A. Trennert, Jr., *Alternative to Extinction* (1975). For the period of the Civil War, government policy can best be followed in Edmund Jefferson Danziger, Jr., *Indians and Bureaucrats* (1974). For the post-Civil War era see Loring Benson Priest, *Uncle Sam's Stepchildren* (1942), and Henry E. Fritz, *The Movement for Indian Assimilation* (1963).

Of books on the Indian wars, there are many. For a general treatment, Robert M. Utley's two volumes are the logical place to begin: *Frontiersmen in Blue: The United States Army and the Indian, 1848–1865* (1967), and *Frontier Regulars: The United States Army and the Indian, 1866–1890* (1973). William H. Leckie, *The Military Conquest of the Southern Plains* (1963), is good, and Donald J. Berthrong, *The Southern Cheyennes* (1963), relates the experience of one of that section's most important tribes. Dan L. Thrapp, *The Conquest of Apacheria* (1967), and Frank McNitt, *Navajo Wars* (1972), are valuable for those Indians, although McNitt's volume only carries the story to 1861. Alvin M. Josephy, Jr., *The Nez Perce Indians and the Openings of the Northwest* (1965), and Keith A. Murray, *The Modocs and Their War* (1959), are the best sources for those two conflicts. Among the books on generals, three deserve particular notice: Robert G. Athearn, *William Tecumseh Sherman and the Settlement of the West* (1956); Richard N. Ellis, *General Pope and U.S. Indian Policy* (1970); James T. King, *War Eagle: A Life of General Eugene A. Carr* (1963).

CHAPTER V

As the time periods for chapters iv and v overlap, many of the works cited for chapter iv apply here also, particularly Priest, *Uncle Sam's Stepchildren,* and Fritz, *The Movement for Indian Assimilation.* These should be supplemented by Francis Paul Prucha, *American Indian Policy in Crisis: Christian Reformers and the Indian, 1865–1900* (1976), which is an excellent synthesis and broader than the subtitle suggests.

American Indians

Studies of particular tribes abound. Typical in their approach are John C. Ewers, *The Blackfeet* (1958); A. M. Gibson, *The Chickasaws* (1971); Donald J. Berthrong, *The Cheyenne and Arapaho Ordeal: Reservation and Agency Life in the Indian Territory, 1875–1907* (1976); and my own *United States–Comanche Relations: The Reservation Years* (1976). For the career of an outstanding Sioux, see James C. Olson, *Red Cloud and the Sioux Problem* (1965). Robert M. Utley, *The Last Days of the Sioux Nation* (1963), is the best account of the Ghost Dance and its tragic aftermath among those people.

Clark Wissler, *Indian Cavalcade* (1938), reprinted as *Red Man Reservations* (1971), is an excellent picture of reservation life around 1900. My *Indian Police and Judges* (1966) expands on one of his topics. A sympathetic portrayal of the founder of the Indian school at Carlisle is Elaine Goodale Eastman, *Pratt: the Red Man's Moses* (1935). Angie Debo, *And Still the Waters Run* (1940), documents the defrauding of the Five Civilized Tribes since the application to them of the Dawes Act.

CHAPTER VI

Hazel W. Hertzberg, *The Search for an American Indian Identity* (1971), surveys the development of modern Pan-Indianism. The very important role of education, 1928–1973, is the subject of Margaret Szasz, *Education and the American Indian* (1974).

There is no single study devoted to Indian policy in the twentieth century. Nor do most of the tribal studies devote much space to the period. The Navajo, however, have received the attention their population and general importance merit. Lawrence C. Kelly, *The Navajo Indians and Federal Indian Policy, 1900–1935* (1968), was the pioneering work on that subject. Donald L. Parman, *The Navajos and the New Deal* (1976), carried the story through World War II. For the career of the architect of the Indian New Deal, see Kenneth R. Philp, *John Collier's Crusade for Indian Reform, 1920–1954* (1977), an objective treatment of a difficult subject. D'Arcy McNickle, *Indian Man: A Life of Oliver La Farge* (1971), deals with a man active in Indian causes and a sometime ally of Collier.

For the Red Power movement, two early accounts were Stan

Suggested Reading

Steiner, *The New Indian* (1968), and a documentary history collected by Alvin M. Josephy, Jr., *Red Power* (1971). Vine Deloria, Jr., *Custer Died for Your Sins* (1969), is both provocative and amusing. *The Road to Wounded Knee* (1974), by Robert Burnette and John Koster, is polemical, but valuable because of Burnette's personal involvement in Rosebud Reservation politics and the march on Washington in 1972.

Two works on federal programs for Indians that are good—despite their cute titles—are Sar A. Levitan and Barbara Hetrick, *Big Brother's Indian Programs—with Reservations* (1971), and the update on that, Sar A. Levitan and William B. Johnson, *Indian Giving: Federal Programs for Native Americans* (1975). Alan L. Sorkin, *American Indians and Federal Aid* (1971), should also be consulted on this topic.

Through the collection of oral history and the publication of tribally sponsored studies, Indians are becoming more involved in the writing of their history. Three books are illustrative of this long overdue development: Joseph H. Cash and Herbert T. Hoover, eds., *To Be an Indian: An Oral History* (1971); Alvina Quam, trans., *The Zunis: Self-Portrayals* (1972); and Floyd O'Neil, ed., *The Southern Utes* (1972). For an Indian viewpoint on Menominee and Klamath termination, as well as related topics, see Kirke Kickingbird and Karen Ducheneaux, *One Hundred Million Acres* (1973).

Index

Adams, John Quincy, 71, 74
Akwesasne Notes, 172
Alabama-Coushattas, 163
Alaskan natives, 168
Albany Conference, 20
Alcatraz, 171
Alcoholism, 160
Aleuts, 168
American Civil Liberties Union, 155
American Indian Chicago Conference, 171
American Indian Defense Association, 155
American Indian Movement, 171–72
Amherst, Lord Jeffrey, 23, 25
Anderson, Mad Bear, 171
Apaches, 111, 126; acquire metal weapons, 6; at war, 93, 95, 105, 106, 112; end resistance, 114
Arapahoes, 107, 108, 113, 116, 131
Astor, John Jacob, 66
Atkin, Edmund, 21
Atkinson, General Henry, 73

Baltimore, Lord, 11
Banks, Dennis, 171
Baptists, 89, 128
Battles: Adobe Walls, 114; Fallen Timbers, 52, 53; Horseshoe Bend, 60; Po.nt Pleasant, 28; Pea Ridge, 101–2; Thames, 63; Tippecanoe, 58; Washita, 113, 118
Benton, Thomas Hart, 67, 69, 99
Black Hawk, 62, 72
Black Hawk War, 72–73, 82
Black Hills, 117
Black Kettle, 107
Blackfeet, 94, 116, 125
Bland, Dr. T. A., 124
Blue Jacket, 50
Board of Indian Commissioners, 111–12, 154
Bouquet, Colonel Henry, 25
Bozeman Trail, 108 ff.
Braddock, General Edward, 21, 22
Brant, Joseph, 42, 52, 56; in the Revo ution, 33, 35, 38
Brant, Mary, 18, 33
Bright Eyes, 122

Index

Bureau of Indian Affairs, 67, 159
Burgoyne, General John, 36
Burke Act, 145

Calhoun, John C., 68, 71, 74, 97
Camp Apache, 126
Canonchet, 14
Captain Jack, 115
Carlisle Indian School, 135–36
Carson, Kit, 105–6
Carter, Jimmy, 170
Cass, Lewis, 62, 68, 71
Catholics, 11, 127, 128
Cayugas, 53
Century of Dishonor, A, 123
Cherokees, 7, 40, 45, 46, 49, 51, 57, 70, 99; losses in French and Indian War, 23; tricked by surveyors, 28; in the Revolution, 32; removal, 55, 73–76, 80–81; in the Creek War, 60; in the Civil War, 100–104; on severalty, 142–43
Cheyennes, 113, 116, 118, 122; Sand Creek Massacre, 107–8
Chickasaws, 3, 32, 46, 51, 55, 61; removed, 73, 86; in the Civil War, 100, 103
Chippewas, 3, 83, 141
Chivington, Colonel J. M., 108
Choctaws, 38, 46, 51, 57, 61, 87; character, 3–4; in the Creek War, 60; removed, 73; in the Civil War, 100, 103
Circus Indians, 149
Citizenship, 141, 145, 148
Civil War, 100 ff.
Civilian Conservation Camps, 154
Civilization Fund, 87, 90
Clark, George Rogers, 37
Clark, William, 62
Clarkson, Bishop R. H., 128
Cleveland, Grover, 141–42, 143
Clum, John P., 137
College of William and Mary, 10
Collier, John, 155 ff., 160
Comancheros, 113
Comanches, 3, 93, 94, 95, 106, 108,

139; trouble with immigrant Indians, 86, 87; end resistance, 113–14
Committee of One Hundred, 152
Cornplanter, 53
Cornstalk, 28
Council Fire, 124
Courts of Indian Offenses, 137, 138–39
Crazy Horse, 116, 118, 119
Creeks, 23, 41, 45, 51, 57, 72, 73, 129, 137, 143; Oglethorpe's prestige with, 11–12; in the Revolution, 32, 38; McGillivray's negotiations, 46–48; Creek War, 59–61; removal, 78–80; in the Civil War, 100–104
Crees, 6
Croghan, George, 21, 26
Crows, 3, 95
Custer, George A., 113, 116–18

Dartmouth College, 35
Davis, Jefferson, 105
Dawes, Henry L., 141
Dawes Commission, 146
Dawes Severalty Act of 1887, 141 ff.
Declaration of Independence, 31
Deer, Ada, 164
Delaware Prophet, 24–25, 53, 57
Delawares, 24–25, 35, 51, 98
Deloria, Vine, Jr., 170–71
Detroit, 25, 37, 62, 63
Dieskau, Baron Ludwig August, 21
Dinwiddie, Governor Robert, 19–20
Diseases, 7, 12, 25, 94, 151–52
Douglas, Stephan A., 97
Dragging Canoe, 32, 49
Dreamers, 130
Dull Knife, 122
Dustin, Hannah, 17
Dutch Reformed Church, 111

Education, at William and Mary, 10–11; early agency schools, 87–88, 90–91; in late nineteenth cen-

Index

tury, 134–37; improvements in Hoover administration, 154; John Collier's recommendations, 155–56
Eisenhower, Dwight D., 161–62
Eliot, John, 12
Elliot, Senator James, 68
Emerson, Ralph Waldo, 70
Episcopalians, 127, 128, 129
Eskimos, 168
Everett, Edward, 70

Factory system, 45, 58, 66–67
Fetterman Massacre, 110
Five Civilized Tribes, 88, 99, 141, 144; slavery among, 90; in the Civil War, 100–104; resist severalty, 142–43; *see also*, Cherokees, Creeks, Seminoles, Choctaws, Chickasaws
Forbes, General John, 23
Foreman, Grant, 78
Fort Mims Massacre, 59–60
Forts: Atkinson, 95; Dearborn, 62, 64; Gibson, 80; Kearney, 94; Laramie, 94, 95; Lyon, 107; Pitt, 24, 25; Recovery, 52; William Henry, 21
Foxes, *see* Sacs and Foxes
Franklin, Benjamin, 20, 36
Frelinghuysen, Theodore, 70
French and Indian War, 16, 19 ff.

Gadsden Purchase, 93
Gall, 116, 118
Gallup, N. M., 160
Gates, General Horatio, 36
General Federation of Women's Clubs, 155
Geronimo, 114
Ghost Dance, 129, 130–34
Girard, Forrest J., 170
Grant, Ulysses S., 110–11
Guardianship, 144–45

Hamilton, Lieutenant-Governor Henry, 36

Hampton Institute, 135
Handsome Lake, 53
Hare, Bishop William Hobart, 128, 147
Harmar, General Josiah, 49, 50, 51
Harrison, William Henry, 55, 69, 119; and Tecumseh, 56–58; in the War of 1812, 62, 63
Haverhill, Mass., 17
Hawkins, Benjamin, 48, 59, 61
Hayes, Ira, 160
Henry, Patrick, 27, 34
Hodge, Frederick Webb, 152
Hoover, Herbert, 153, 161
Hoover Commission, 161
Horses, impact on Indian culture, 4–5, 92, 106
Houston, Sam, 98
Hurons, 6

Ickes, Harold, 155
Indian Citizenship Committee, 123
Indian Claims Commission, 168
Indian Historian, 172
Indian police, 132, 137–38
Indian Reorganization Act of 1834, 67
Indian Rights Association, 124, 155
Indian Self-Determination and Education Assistance Act of 1975, 169
Industrialization, 165–67
Institute for Government Research, 153
Interior Department, 109, 111
Iroquois, 15, 27, 53; establish an empire, 6; in the French wars, 16 ff.; in the Revolution, 32 ff.; *see also* Mohawks, Senecas, Tuscaroras, Oneidas, and Cayugas
Isatai, 130

Jackson, Andrew, 60–61, 119; policies as president, 72, 73, 75
Jackson, Helen Hunt, 123, 140
James I, 9

Index

Jay's Treaty, 51
Jefferson, Thomas, 53–55, 58
Johnson, Guy, 32, 33, 35
Johnson, Lyndon, 166
Johnson, William, 18, 21, 32, 33
Johnson-O'Malley Act, 160–61
Joseph, Chief, 115–16, 128
Joseph, Old, 115–16

Kaws, 98
Kearney, Major Phil, 94
Keokuk, 72
Key, Francis Scott, 79
Kickapoos, 101
Kieft, Governor Willem, 15
King George's War, 16, 18
King Philip's War, 14
King William's War, 16
Kiowas, 3, 94, 106, 108, 143; end resistance, 113–14
Kirkland, Samuel, 33
Klamaths, 163–64
Knox, Henry, 43–44

Lake Mohonk Conference, 124
Language groups, 3
LaSalle, Robert Cavalier, 6
Leasing Indian land, 144
Leupp, Francis E., 147
Light Horse, 137
Lincoln, Abraham, 73
Little Abraham, 35
Little Antelope, 107
Little Crow, 104–5
Little Mountain, 143
Little Turtle, 50, 52
Little Wolf, 122
Logan, Chief, 28
Lord Dunmore's War, 26, 27–28

McCrea, Jenny, 36
McGillivray, Alexander, 45, 60; on British payroll, 32; tactics and character, 41; influence, 46–47, 49
McIntosh, William, 60
Mackinac, see Michilimackinac

McNickle, D'Arcy, 171
Madison, James, 53, 61
Mandans, 94
Manypenny, George W., 127
Marshall, John, 54, 75
Mary, 11–12
Mather, Cotton, 14
Meacham, Alfred B., 115, 123
Means, Russell, 171
Menominees, 163–64
Meriam, Dr. Lewis, 153
Meriam Report, 153, 155
Methodists, 89
Miamis, 19, 50, 51, 98
Michilimackinac, 25, 62, 64
Miles, General Nelson A., 108
Mingos, 28
Mission Indians, 8, 17, 96
Missionary activity: in Virginia, 9; in Maryland, 11; in New England, 12; Catholic progress, 20; in the Revolution, 31; as a civilizing agent, 43, 89–91, 127–29; see also the different denominations
Modoc War, 112, 114, 115, 123
Mohawks, 18, 35, 53
Monroe, James, 71
Mount Rushmore, 171
Myer, Dillon S., 161, 165

Nana, 114
Narragansetts, 13, 14
National Association of Indian Affairs, 155
National Congress of American Indians, 159, 170–71
National Indian Association, 123
National Indian Defense Association, 124
National Indian Youth Council, 171
Native American Church, 150
Native American Rights Fund, 173
Navajos, 93, 95, 168; acquire horses and sheep, 4, 5; end resistance, 105–6; attitude toward the dead, 152, 159
Neutral Ground (Iowa), 82, 83

Index

Nez Percés, 5, 112, 114, 122; outbreak of 1877, 115–16
Niagara, 37
Nixon, Richard M., 166
Northwest Posts, 41, 51, 52

Oglethorpe, James Edward, 11, 12
Ohio Company of Virginia, 20
Oil Indians, 147
Omahas, 84
Oneidas, 33
Opechancanough, 10, 11
Ordinance of 1787, 42
Osages, 62, 86, 87
Osceola, 77
Ottawas, 25
Ouray, 115
Outing system, 135–36

Paiutes, 116, 130–31
Pancoast, Henry S., 124
Pan-Indian movement, 150, 157–58
Papagos, 3, 95
Parker, Ely S., 112
Parker, Quanah, 114, 139
Passamaquoddys, 173
Pautapety, 130
Pawnees, 3, 6, 62, 90, 98; between immigrant Indians and the Sioux, 86; serve as scouts, 148
Peace Commission of 1867, 112
Penn, William, 15, 16
Penobscots, 173
Pequot War of 1637, 13
Peyote cult, 129–30, 150
Philip, 14, 56
Pickawillany, 19
Pilgrims, 7, 12, 14, 15
Pimas, 95, 160
Plenty of Horses, 135
Plumb, Senator Preston B., 123
Plymouth Rock, 171
Pocahontas, 9
Poinkia, 130
Poncas, 122
Pontiac, 25–26, 56
Porter, Pleasant, 143–44

Powhatan, 9–10
Potawatomis, 58
Prairie du Chien, 63, 64
Pratt, Richard H., 135–36, 139, 141
Presbyterians, 89, 128
Princeton University, 35
Proclamation of 1763, 26
Prophet's Town, 58
Pueblos, 3, 95, 152
Purchas, Reverend Samuel, 10
Puritans, 12, 14
Pushmataha, 60

Quaker Policy, 110–11, 124, 127
Quakers, 18, 19, 124, 129, 153; treat Indians equitably, 15–16
Quapaws, 138
Queen Anne's War, 16, 18

Race prejudice, 8, 12, 173
Ramona, 123
Rector, Elias, 100
Red Cloud, 108, 109, 119, 124, 133
Red Cross, 154
Red Jacket, 53
Red Power, 170 ff.
Red River War, 112–14
Red Sticks, 60
Relocation Program, 165–66
Removal Policy, origin, 54–56; implemented, 66 ff.; Removal Bill of 1830, 72; for Kansas Indians, 102–4
Rhoads, Charles J., 153
Rockefeller, John D., Jr., 153
Rolfe, John, 9
Roosevelt, Franklin D., 155, 156
Rosebud Agency, 127
Ross, John, 60, 74, 101
Rutgers University, 111

Sacs and Foxes, 3, 18, 57, 82; in the War of 1812, 63; removed, 72–73; fight plains Indians, 86
St. Clair, Arthur, 42, 49, 50, 51
San Carlos, 126
Sand Creek Massacre, 107–8

Index

Satank, 113, 114

Satanta, 113, 114

Scattergood, J. Henry, 153

Scott, Winfield, 73, 80

Seaton, Fred A., 163

Self-determination, 166 ff.

Seminoles, 3, 61, 72, 73, 100, 150, 163; Seminole War and Removal, 76–77, 87

Senecas, 53, 112

Severalty, 112, 121, 138; theory behind, 43, 140 ff.; opposition to, 153, 154, 155

Seward, William, 100

Seymour, Flora, 156

Shawnee Prophet, 53, 56–58

Shawnees, 27, 28, 50, 51, 58

Sheridan, Phil, 113, 119

Sherman, William Tecumseh, 109, 118

Shoshones, 119, 148

Sioux, 3, 57, 62, 83, 84, 86, 95, 112, 124, 127, 149; Uprising of 1862, 84, 104–5; and Bozeman Trail, 108 ff.; defeat Custer, 116–18; Ghost Dance, 131–33

Sitting Bull, 116, 118, 138, 148–49; defeats Custer, 118; death, 132

Six Nations, see Iroquois

Skenandoa, 33

Slavery, Indian, 14, 17; Negro, 76, 90

Smiley, Albert K., 124

Smohollah, 116, 130

Society of Jesus, 11

Soldier societies, 137

Spotted Tail, 121

Squanto, 12

Standing Rock Agency, 132

Sullivan, General John, 37–38

Sullivan, Mark, 152

Supreme Court, 54, 75

Taylor, Zachary, 63, 73, 77

Tax, Sol, 171

Tecumseh, 53, 59; opposes Harrison, 56–58; in the War of 1812, 62, 63

Tenskwatawa, see Shawnee Prophet

Termination, 160 ff.

Tibbles, T. H., 122

Tocqueville, Alexis de, 70

Tourism, 165–67

Trade, 8, 11, 15, 19, 20, 22, 23, 24, 26, 31, 33, 40, 44–45, 113; impact, 6–7, 16–17, 85, 106; as a factor in producing the Revolution, 28–29

Trade and Intercourse Acts, 44, 67

Trail of Tears, 78

Treaties: Echota, 76; Fort Jackson, 60; Fort Laramie, 95; Fort Wayne, 57, 58; Ghent, 63, 65; Greenville, 52, 62; Guadalupe Hidalgo, 92, 93; New York, 47; San Lorenzo, 49; Creek (1832), 78

Tuscaroras, 33

University of New Mexico, 173

University of Oklahoma, 173

Utes, 3, 112, 114; War of 1879, 115

Van Buren, Martin, 81

Vattel, 8

Victoria, 114

Victoria, Franciscus de, 8

Virginia Company, 9

Voltaire, 16

Wampanoags, 14, 29

War of 1812, 58 ff.

Wasaja, 172

Washakie, 119

Washington, George, 27, 34, 37, 43, 45

Watie, Stand, 101, 102

Watkins, Senator Arthur V., 160

Wayne, Anthony, 49, 51–52

Weatherford, William, 60

Welsh, Herbert, 124, 152

Wheeler-Howard (Indian Reorganization) Act, 156–58, 160–62

Index

Whipple, Bishop Henry Benjamin, 128, 129
Whitepath, 74
Wilbur, Ray Lyman, 153
Williams, Roger, 12, 13
Wilson, Jack, *see* Wovoka
Winnebagos, 2, 58; Winnebago War, 81; removal, 81–85
Wirt, William, 75

Worcester vs. *Georgia*, 75
Work, Herbert, 152–53
World War I, 148
World War II, 158
Wounded Knee, 133, 172
Wovoka, 130–31
Wyandots, 51

Yankton, South Dakota, 174